# Communication in the Language Classroom

Also published in
**Oxford Handbooks for Language Teachers**

# Communication
# in the Language Classroom

*Tony Lynch*

Oxford University Press

# OXFORD

UNIVERSITY PRESS

Great Clarendon Street, Oxford OX2 6DP

Oxford University Press is a department of the University of Oxford.
It furthers the University's objective of excellence in research, scholarship,
and education by publishing worldwide in

Oxford New York

Auckland Cape Town Dar es Salaam Hong Kong Karachi
Kuala Lumpur Madrid Melbourne Mexico City Nairobi
New Delhi Shanghai Taipei Toronto

With offices in

Argentina Austria Brazil Chile Czech Republic France Greece
Guatemala Hungary Italy Japan Poland Portugal Singapore
South Korea Switzerland Thailand Turkey Ukraine Vietnam

OXFORD and OXFORD ENGLISH are registered trade marks of
Oxford University Press in the UK and in certain other countries

© Tony Lynch 1996

The moral rights of the author have been asserted

Database right Oxford University Press (maker)

First published 1996

2016 2015 2014 2013
10

ISBN : 978 0 19 433522 5

Typeset by Wyvern Typesetting Ltd., Bristol
in Adobe Garamond

Printed in China

To Horsham and Them

# CONTENTS

# ACKNOWLEDGEMENTS

The seeds for this book were sown in a course on 'Simplification in the Language Classroom', which I taught in 1991 at the TESOL Mediterranean Institute at ESADE, Barcelona. The response of the participants was an important influence on my decision to write the book, so my thanks to Ahmed El-Shamy, Marilou Engels, Maria Dolors García Bosch, Montserrat Pérez Pérez, Sofía Rodríguez-Torres, Jamie Drury, Susan Hindson, Imelda Commons Callaghan, Ulziijargal Sanjaasurengin, Basem Saheb Tamini, and Walid Abu Halaweh, both for their enthusiasm and their questions.

Two years later I had the opportunity to try out some of my ideas in a rather different setting, in a series of in-service workshops for Indian secondary school and college teachers of English. I am grateful to the Directors of the three institutions concerned, for their help and hospitality: Mrs Harjit Vasudev of the Regional Institute of English in Chandigarh, Professor D.K. Ray of the English Language Teaching Institute in Bhubaneswar, and Professor B. Banerjee of the Institute of English in Calcutta. That time in India confirmed my view that, when it comes to changing the way languages are taught and learnt, the attitudes of individuals matter at least as much as the resources of institutions.

The third group of people whose help I would like to acknowledge are the students and teachers at the Institute for Applied Language Studies of the University of Edinburgh, with whom I have worked since 1980. I owe a particular debt to those colleagues who allowed me to record their classes—Kenneth Anderson, Wendy Ball, Jacqueline Gollin, Jennifer Higham, Cliona McGowan, Jane Palfery, and Brian Parkinson—and to the many other teachers and learners of English who took part in experiments for my doctoral research in Scotland and in Portugal.

As always, the final shape of the book bears the influences of a number of readers. Mauricéa Lima Lynch and Edwin Lynch proofread (and more) far beyond the call of Christmas; Henry Widdowson and two anonymous reviewers provided detailed comments on the original manuscript; Eileen Dwyer and Miki Inoué gave me valuable help with points of Arabic and Japanese translation. Last but not least, my thanks to Anne Conybeare and Julia Sallabank of Oxford University Press, for encouraging initial growth and for their advice on weeding and pruning.

TONY LYNCH
*Edinburgh 1995*

The publishers and author thank the following for their kind permission to reproduce extracts and adaptations from works for which they hold the copyright:

The BBC for adaptations from an interview with Malcolm Rifkind in the *Today* programme (BBC Radio 4 1985), *The Six O'Clock News* (BBC1 TV 1985), *John Craven's Newsround* (BBC1 TV 1985), *Medicine Now* (BBC Radio 4 3.8.1994), and *The Moral Maze* (BBC Radio 4 1.9.1994)

Cambridge University Press for extracts from G. Brown and G. Yule: *Discourse Analysis* (1983), C. Chaudron: *Second Language Classrooms* (1988), and T. Lynch and K. Anderson: *Study Speaking* (1992)

Croom Helm (International Thomson Publishing Services Ltd) for an extract from G. McGregor and R. White: *The Art of Listening*

ELT Mov for an extract from M. Kundu: *Teacher's Handbook for Progressive English*

HarperCollins for an extract form N. Wymer: *The Kon-Tiki Expedition* (1973)

Hüber Holzmann for an extract from *Englisch für berufsbildende Schulen: Grundlehrgang* (1975)

Longman Group UK for two illustrations from J. B. Heaton: *Composition through Pictures* (1966)

Vanessa Luk for an extract from 'Developing Interactional Listening Strategies in a Foreign Language: a Study of Two Classroom Approaches' (1994)

Newbury House for an extract from D. Larsen-Freeman: *Discourse Analysis in Second Language Research*

The *Observer* for a book review by Lucy Tuck taken from 'Christmas Books' 20.11.1994

Oxford University Press for an adaptation of a figure from A. Anderson and T. Lynch: *Listening* (1988), and for two figures from *Applied Linguistics* (1986); Oxford University Press and Guy Cook for an extract from *Discourse* (1989)

Brian Parkinson for permission to adapt an extract from 'Classroom Processes' course materials
Penguin Books for permission to adapt biodata on Ernest Hemingway from *For Whom the Bell Tolls*
The publishers of *RELC Journal* for an extract from an article by S. Cotterall (1990)
Dr A. Shehadeh for an extract from 'Comprehension and Performance in Second Language Acquisition: A Study of Second Language Learners' Production of Modified Comprehensible Output' (1991)
University of Edinburgh for a map of city centre shops
Professor H. G. Widdowson for an extract from *Teaching Language as Communication* published by Oxford University Press (1978)

Although every effort has been made to trace and contact copyright holders before publication, this has not been possible in some cases. We apologize for any apparent infringement of copyright and if notified, the publisher will be pleased to rectify any errors or omissions at the earliest opportunity.

# INTRODUCTION

> If you know how something works, you can begin to work out how to interfere with it.
> (Professor Lewis Wolpert, BBC Radio 4: 27 May 1995)

As teachers we are probably reluctant to think of what we do professionally as 'interference'; 'intervention' sounds better. This book looks at how communication works, since knowing how people succeed and fail in their efforts to communicate can help us to intervene to make learners' use of language more effective. Part One explores the characteristics of natural spoken interaction that we should take into account in teaching a language and in evaluating learners' performances. In Part Two I suggest various ways of encouraging interaction through classroom tasks in the four traditional language skills—listening, speaking, reading, and writing.

## 'It wouldn't work here because ...'

A common reaction to any suggestion for change is to find reasons for keeping things as they are. Faced with recommendations for changes to classroom practice, teachers may respond by pointing out differences between their own circumstances and those of the person making the suggestion, or between theory and practice.

## Differences between teaching situations

In 1993 I was preparing for a series of workshops for English teachers in India, on the topic of 'teaching for communicative competence'. I expected to find that some teachers would be resistant to change and would argue that the materials and techniques I was going to demonstrate were impracticable in their teaching situation, for reasons such as class size and lack of resources.

In fact, the response I encountered was very different. The debate that arose was not between me, the outside speaker, and local teachers, but between those teachers who already used communicative techniques like the ones I had presented and those who did not. The unpersuaded teachers raised objections such as 'it might work here in the city, but it wouldn't work in our rural schools' and 'it might work in private schools, but it wouldn't work in government schools'. As I listened to their arguments, I became more convinced that what really persuades people to make professional change is the practical experience of trying out something themselves. So this book offers you the experience at second hand of seeing how various classroom tasks worked, so that you can judge for yourself whether and how to adapt them to your own teaching situation.

## *Differences between theory and practice*

Part One of the book reports the findings of research into interaction involving language learners, and discusses their implications for the design of interaction-orientated classroom tasks. Many teachers are sceptical of research and researchers, and rightly so; there is no guarantee that any specific research finding necessarily helps teachers to teach or learners to learn. In a recent *TESOL Quarterly* article, Mark Clarke argued that, no matter how carefully researchers try to reproduce the conditions of normal classroom teaching in their experiments, 'the conclusions they draw are, by necessity, less complex than the reality that teachers confront every day' (Clarke 1994: 16). He illustrated that complexity by listing ten constraints on teachers' decision-making in a typical day: personal philosophy, physical space, time, available resources, interpersonal and institutional factors, community considerations, syllabus and assessment requirements, and classroom routine.

Another reason for the lack of connection between academic research and teachers' lives is that the assumptions and needs of the two professional worlds are different. Researchers want to make their findings generalizable to other contexts; what individual teachers need to know is which, if any, of those findings are 'particularizable'—that is, can they be made relevant to their own situations? This always requires adaptation.

> We cannot expect that the experience and experiments of other people in other places occupied with other problems will produce answers off the peg which will fit our particular requirements.
> (Widdowson 1990: 27)

In Part Two of the book I discuss how some research findings have been, or could be, translated into practical teaching techniques for the teaching of the four skills. The purpose in doing so is not to sell ready-made solutions, but to offer examples for you to evaluate. It may be that some suggestions could be adapted for your local context, and that 'it wouldn't work here because . . .' will give way to 'it might work here if . . .'.

## *Recordings used in the book*

It follows from what I have said so far that it is not possible to describe a 'universal' language classroom. What I do in this book is to illustrate the teaching of the four traditional skills with extracts from recordings I have made over a period of twelve years or so. I stress that these are samples, and not models of what to do or not to do.

Most of the examples come from English classes that I have observed at the Institute for Applied Language Studies (IALS) of the University of Edinburgh; a few were made in the course of an experiment which involved teachers and learners talking in a non-classroom setting. In the text I make clear which extracts come from observation data and which from experimental data, because I agree with Mark Clarke that there are important differences between 'the messy business of actual language use' (Clarke 1994: 15) in everyday teaching and a relatively controlled experiment.

## *Transcripts*

Where I have used a transcript from published work, I have kept to the form of the transcription used by the original author(s). In the case of my own transcripts I broadly follow conventions used by Brown and Yule (1983): speakers are identified by a single letter (T always being the teacher); pauses are represented by '+', '+ +', or '+ + +', depending on their relative duration; phrases in italics provide a comment on events, for example, laughter. (As you will see in due course, laughter is quite common in the recordings—for reasons you will have to work out for yourself.)

# PART ONE

## Input, interaction, and negotiation

# 1 COMMUNICATING INSIDE AND OUTSIDE THE CLASSROOM

## Introduction

Communication involves enabling someone else to understand what we want to tell them, what is often referred to as our message. We probably tend to think of a message as being factual, and it is true that we *can* communicate facts, but in many everyday situations we also hope to communicate our opinions and emotions. As well as informing our listener or reader, we may hope to amuse, entertain, or mislead, for example.

As language teachers we also have to guard against assuming that communication necessarily requires the use of language; the sign showing a lit cigarette with a red line through it 'tells' us that smoking is not allowed. In the case of a foreign setting, it does so more effectively than, for example, the words 'DILARANG MEROKOK' would by themselves.

Communication involves an audience. In the case of one-way spoken communication such as a radio broadcast, a member of the audience can justifiably be referred to as a 'listener', since they have no opportunity to respond or to intervene. However, in two-way communication such as face-to-face conversation, the social role of 'listening' often involves a considerable amount of talking. For this reason I will be using the word 'partner' to refer to someone engaged in spoken communication.

One term used to describe the process by which the partners in a conversation reach agreement is *interaction*. As soon as we look at examples of real conversations we see just how much people collaborate in achieving communication. In Example 1.1 two university lecturers are discussing how the way you look can affect the way you feel.

*Example 1.1*

    **B** I think if your physical appearance is em sort of neat and + well-controlled and so on this gives at least a superficial + feeling that one's going to give a neat and well-controlled performance

L    that's right + do you know I remember something that Gill said
+ and it's now suppose er + er eight years ago + when + em +
what's that Russian chap's name who was here for a while
B    Shaumyan
L    Shaumyan yeah + when he was here + em I gave a seminar on . . .
(Brown and Yule 1983: 149)

The two partners share the duties, so to speak, in the interaction. Speaker
B initiates the topic of the relationship between appearance and confidence and, when B's turn is complete, L shows his agreement by 'that's
right' and takes up B's point by embarking on an anecdote to support B's
view. There then occurs an example of what is termed conversational
*repair.* L indicates there is a problem—he cannot remember the Russian
visitor's name. Speaker B steps in with the relevant information and the
conversation continues.

Another form of collaborative repair is correction, either of an error of
form (e.g. pronunciation, grammar, and word choice) or content. In the
1970s North American researchers found that English conversation
appears to operate on an unspoken principle that self-correction is prefer-
able to other-correction, i.e. being corrected by the partner (Schegloff
1979). Some of the characteristics of correction are illustrated in Example
1.2, which comes from the commentary of a televised football match.
Commentator B is pointing out that the manager of one of the teams has
already used the two substitutes allowed under the rules of this particular European competition.

*Example 1.2*
B    so now he could have a real problem + + he's used all his
substitutes and + if this injury is as serious as + + uh
T    um + + + all of them?
B    as it looks + + well there's nobody left to come on
T    hm but + + when you say ALL + + + I mean he's only allowed      5
the two Brian
B    quite right thank you Terry + BOTH I should say + + so
Arsenal could have a real problem here now . . .

In that episode T wants to point out to B that his use of 'all' implies that
the Arsenal manager has used three substitutes rather than two. In doing
so, T adopts three of the typical devices found in correction in English
conversation:

– he leaves two long pauses (in lines 3 and 5) to allow B the chance to
notice his error
– he queries what B has said by repeating it with rising intonation ('all
of them?' in line 3)

– he softens the correction by saying 'I mean . . .' (line 5) and also by using B's first name (line 6).

So what on the surface is a self-correction ('BOTH I should say') has in fact been achieved through the prompting of the other speaker. This is a trivial but typical example of 'getting something corrected without correcting it yourself—a relatively complex interactive process and one we probably take for granted in everyday communication.

Repair covers a wider range of behaviour than simply correction. It may involve the need to clarify a word or expression which is correct and appropriate, but happens to be unfamiliar to the other person. For this reason, it is now more common to refer to the resolution of communication problems as *negotiation of meaning*. The word *negotiation* highlights the give-and-take between conversational partners, compared with the mechanical overtones of *repair*.

The next two examples show how, even in our first language, misunderstandings may need to be sorted out through cooperative negotiation. In Example 1.3 one speaker uses a two-word expression that his partner has not come across before.

*Example 1.3*
    **A**  what have you got to do this afternoon?
    **B**  oh I'm going to repair the child bar
    **A**  what do you mean CHILD bar?
    **B**  uh it's a metal bar that goes acr. . . has to be fixed from one side
        of the car I mean from one side of the back seat to the other for
        the BABY seat to go on
    **A**  Ah . . .
(Cook 1989: 55)

When A indicates he does not understand 'child bar', B feels obliged to provide an explanation. We can tell that B seems to assume that A must be unfamiliar with the object in question, since he begins his explanation with 'it's *a* metal bar that . . .'. If B had thought A was familiar with the object but did not know the name for it, he would probably have explained it as 'it's *the* metal bar that . . .'.

In Example 1.4 the problem is rather different: here it is one speaker's use of an extremely rare academic word ('inanition') that leads to negotiation.

*Example 1.4*
    **EP**  what we've got now is inanition
    **MB**  in an . . .?
    **EP**  inanition

MB  what's inanition?
JD  that's one to add to the five hundred thousand words in the
     English language
EP  it's + not going anywhere + very slowly + + ok?
MB  ok
(*The Moral Maze*, BBC Radio 4: 1 September 1994)

That exchange arose in a philosophical discussion among academics, who might have been expected to know even the more obscure terms in their field. But it is apparently only EP who is familiar with 'inanition'. MB's query 'in an . . .?' may be asked for his own benefit; alternatively, since he is chairing the discussion, it may be that he asks for clarification for the unseen audience. The fact that JD adds her comment about having to add one more word to the stock of English could indicate that she is being ironic at EP's expense, or possibly that she is embarrassed about not knowing the word.

All the examples I have presented so far occurred in conversations between fully competent native speakers of English. The fact that they contained obstacles to communication (a memory lapse, an inappropriate word choice, a novel expression, and an obscure term) does not make them deviant or incompetent interactions; they are typical of a great deal of informal spontaneous talk.

So there are two points to make on the basis of the discussion so far. First, we should always try to compare learners' performances in a foreign language with what we can reasonably expect of competent native speakers, and not assess them in terms of a 'perfect' performance. It is only by taking a realistic view of what language use by native speakers sounds and looks like that we can evaluate interaction in a classroom where the learners are non-native speakers. The second point is that, in real life, people succeed in conversation through interactive collaboration; partners share the burden of making themselves—and each other—understood. This is a topic I will return to in Part Two.

## 'Teacher Talk'

So far we have looked at examples from native conversation. In Chapter 3 I will be examining the ways in which language teachers talk to their students, and in which students talk to each other. In particular I will be focusing on what is called '*Teacher Talk*', that is, the language typically used by teachers in the foreign language classroom. You may have noticed that I have taken care to give the expression capital letters and put it inside quotation marks, suggesting that I want to distance myself from it.

Teachers vary widely in their attitudes to 'Teacher Talk' (both the term and the behaviour it refers to). Some accept that it is a useful device for communicating with students at all levels except the most advanced; others regard it as an important part of the early stages of learning, but believe it should be abandoned as soon as possible; one of my colleagues even claims that she has 'never used it'.

## *Activity*

### Giving explanations

Giving explanations is one of the language functions that might be thought to be more typical of talk inside the classroom than outside. Below are extracts from four different conversations containing explanations, which are underlined. As you read them, decide:

1 whether you think the partners were native or non-native users of English
2 whether they were talking in a classroom, and
3 why one of them felt an explanation was necessary.

*Example 1.5*

    E  well yes funnily enough you know + Gary Sobers to him is + the epitome of of cricket and

    F  ah yes <u>the famous West Indian cricketer</u>

    E  yes

*Example 1.6*

    J  what about the prisoners' allegations of brutality?

    K  well of course it's open to any prisoner to make a complaint to the police or the procurator fiscal + + <u>that's the independent prosecutor in Scotland</u> + + and any complaint would be dealt with on its merits

*Example 1.7*

    M  sorry + you said + + something I didn't catch + what I have written down is + + 'soccer more'?

    N  oh + sophomore + I'm sorry

    M  what is that + can you explain?

    N  in the universities students joining the first year are freshmen + <u>the second year is sophomore</u> + and then junior and senior

    M  aha + so it means second-year student?

    N  yeah

    M  OK

    N  anyway . . .

*Example 1.8*
R    people say it's the oldest most haunted restaurant
S    haunted?
R    <u>haunted is when the ghosts come</u> + whoo-oo-oo-ooh
S    *(laughs)* right
R    right? so . . .

Example 1.5 occurred in an interview recorded for an EFL listening comprehension course (O'Neill and Scott 1974). The interviewer F assumed that the learners would not know who Gary Sobers was, and so he added an explanation for the eventual consumers of the material.

In Example 1.6, speaker K was the Secretary of State for Scotland, who was being interviewed by a London-based reporter for BBC Radio 4. He explained the meaning of the Scottish 'procurator fiscal' for the benefit of the unseen (and predominantly English) audience—as MB did with 'ina-nition' in Example 1.4. Again, the explanation was not intended for the immediate partner.

Examples 1.7 and 1.8 both come from the language classroom, but they differ in terms of who provided the explanation. In 1.7 both speakers were language learners: speaker M asked his fellow student N for help with 'sophomore', a word he had not encountered before and presumably could not understand from context. (Incidentally, since it is a North American word, 'sophomore' would probably also have puzzled most British native speakers). Example 1.8 is in fact the only one of these four extracts to feature a language teacher explaining an unfamiliar word to one of her students.

So the differences between 'Teacher Talk' and talk in other situations are relative; they are differences in how often certain language forms or functions are used, not whether they are used or not. But there are no fundamental differences in the grammatical quality of the language spoken to language learners.

# 'Learner talk'

In one sense, we can also say that the characteristics of conversation between language learners are the same as those involving native speakers. I am referring not to the accuracy of the language used, but to the overall pattern of negotiation of meaning. Two researchers working in Michigan, Evangeline Varonis and Susan Gass, carried out a series of studies comparing interaction between three types of pairs: native–native, native–non-native, and non-native–non-native. They analysed in particular the ways in which the two partners engaged in repair. Varonis and

Gass adopted the term *pushdown* to refer to a point in a conversation at which the talk is 'put on hold' while a problem is sorted out. Perhaps the closest analogy with the pushdown is that of the pause button on a tape recorder, as suggested in Figure 1.1.

*Figure 1.1: A pushdown in conversation* (after Varonis and Gass 1985)

If we apply the pushdown model to Example 1.7, we have the following sequence:

M (sorry)+ you said + + something I didn't catch + what I have      **॥**
written down is + + 'soccer more'?                                  |
N   oh + sophomore + I'm sorry                                      R
M   what is that + can you explain?                                 E
N   in the universities students joining the first year are fresh-  
men + the second year is sophomore + and then junior and           P
senior                                                             A
M   aha + so it means second-year student?                          |
N   yeah                                                            R
M   ok                                                              |
N   (anyway). . .                                                   ▶

There are strong similarities between this example of conversational repair and Example 1.2 (the correction sequence between the two comment-ators): student M identifies the trouble source, 'soccer more', in a softened and unthreatening way: '*sorry* you said something *I didn't catch*'. Student N is also apologetic, for having used a word that a listener is unfamiliar with. The partners work through their negotiation co-operatively until they reach a point where N feels able to signal ('anyway') that he is about to take up the thread of the discourse again.

By comparing interactions in the three partner combinations, Varonis and Gass were able to show that pushdowns leading to negotiation of mean-ing were least frequent between the native speaker pairs and most frequent where both partners were learners of English. Moreover, they found that the greater the similarity between the non-native partners, the less likely they were to need to resolve communication problems through negoti-ation.

At first sight this appears to have negative implications for teachers working with monolingual classes—that is, most teachers, perhaps? They will have a harder task than those who teach students who have a different first language, because interaction between learners (e.g. in pair or group work) is likely to produce less negotiation than in multicultural contexts, with learners from different backgrounds. However, this is where the teacher's professional expertise comes in. In a 'natural' conversation, as Varonis and Gass showed, there may be less need for negotiation when the partners can rely on shared knowledge and experience. So one of the challenges of language teaching in the 'unnatural' classroom setting is to devise or adapt communication tasks in such a way as to require negotiation of meaning in spite of the relative similarity of the learners' background. In Chapters 5 to 8 I suggest some ways in which negotiation can be 'designed in' with this aim in mind.

## Terms for 'negotiation'

There are a number of different terms used to refer to the way in which speakers change what they say in the course of negotiation of meaning in order to make it understandable to their audience. Among the most common are *adjustment, accommodation,* and *simplification.* Although the terms were coined to be used in a neutral way, they may have rather different connotations. For example, they may have different nuances in terms of the degree of change involved: *adjustment* suggests more minor change. They may also reflect the context in which they are used: *accommodation* is more commonly used about spoken language, *simplification* about written texts.

For some people, *accommodation* may have associations with being 'accommodating'—in what a Scottish journalist recently called 'the sort of kindly way the English reserve for foreigners and slow learners' (Moncur 1994). But, as used by academics, accommodation is a neutral term and comes from the field of social psychology. 'Speech accommodation theory' is based on research into the ways in which, in our first language, we adjust what we say and the way we say it according to our relationship with the person we are talking to. Our speech patterns (e.g. accent and vocabulary) tend to converge towards those of a conversational partner with whom we feel empathy or solidarity. Conversely, we are likely to diverge away from those from whom we feel remote or distinct. The theory assumes that we constantly assess our own speech in relation to that of our partner. Seen in this light, we could say that the accommodations made to and by language learners are simply a particular case of a more general phenomenon.

The term *simplification* is ambiguous. It can refer to the adjustment itself (e.g. using a common item such as 'sad' instead of the less common 'depressed') or to the *effect* of the adjustment (whether or not their partner understands the message). Not all intended simplifications result in successful comprehension on the part of the language learner. This is similar to the ambiguity in the way teachers talk about 'correcting', which can refer either to the *act* of correcting, as in

> I corrected her pronunciation of 'south' but she didn't hear me.

or to the successful remedying of a problem:

> It took nearly two terms for me to correct his problems with relative clauses.

A final point about simplification is that it can be achieved in two different ways. A speaker may choose to make the message simpler in *linguistic* terms (e.g. by using simpler language) or in *cognitive* terms (e.g. by offering the listener additional information). These two approaches to adjustment for the listener are known as *restrictive* and *elaborative* simplification, respectively. Below are examples of these simplification types from two university lectures given by the same lecturer to native and non-native students:

*Restrictive simplification*
> *To the native listeners:*        'it's <u>ironic</u>'
> *To the non-native listeners:*    'it <u>seems funny</u>'

> *Native:*       'if you worked hard you would <u>make it</u>'
> *Non-native:*   'if you could work hard, you would <u>be rewarded</u>'

*Elaborative simplification*    (for the non-native listeners)
> 'the beaver is known as a very industrious <u>and busy, uhm, hard working</u> animal'

> 'Canada was booming <u>and expanding and economically rich</u>'
> (Chaudron 1979)

As teachers, we need to be aware that making language simpler for a foreign language learner does not guarantee greater comprehension, as in the example below:

*Example 1.9*
> **Caretaker**  could you give it a shove for me please
> **Student**    uh?
> **Caretaker**  just give it a shove
> **Student**    sorry?
> **Caretaker**  shove it
> **Student**    shove?

> **Caretaker**    *(gestures with his foot)* the door
> **Student**      ah push + yes *(pushes the door open)*

That is my recollection of an incident I witnessed in which an EFL school caretaker was carrying a large reel-to-reel tape recorder and tried to get one of the foreign students to open a sliding door. It was the first time I had noticed that making things simpler linguistically does not always have the intended effect. In this case, restrictive simplification failed because the caretaker had not realized that 'shove' was not in the student's vocabulary.

At the other extreme, elaborative simplification runs the risk of being confusing. The student may get lost in the redundant information supplied by a well-meaning teacher:

> There appear to be pitfalls in an approach to elaboration that would assume that learners will 'pick up' the meanings if enough redundant elaboration is provided. The very opposite may happen, and the learners could 'tune out' what the teacher is saying.
> (Chaudron 1979: 11)

So above all we need to simplify in a way that is appropriate for particular learners. If one route to simplification seems to be blocked, then we have to be prepared to try another. In Chapter 3 I will look at alternative forms of simplification in more detail.

# Comprehension

So far I have considered the process of communication largely from the point of view of the speaker; of course the listener also has a significant part to play. In Chapter 2 I will be analysing some ways in which the listener (or reader) contributes to the process of successful communication, but in this section I would like to look briefly at two general aspects of comprehension: its complexity and its possible role in the development of the learner's competence in the foreign language.

## *Complexity of comprehension*

What is commonly called 'the comprehension process' is really a bundle of different processes: among others, deciphering the sounds the speaker is making, recognizing what they are talking about, inferring things that have been left unsaid, and interpreting what the implications are. A message may be understood on different levels by different listeners. I will take an imaginary example to show just how much mental work a listener may do in attempting to understand even quite a short piece of spoken language.

The British government announces its spending and taxation plans in an annual Budget speech made in the House of Commons. Imagine that a business executive, anxious to hear how the changes might affect her company, misses the speech itself. As she turns on the radio, she hears a speaker saying 'The reduction in National Insurance contributions will do nothing for the unemployed'. Her responses might include any or all of the following (and many more besides):

1 the Government has decided to cut (employers' and employees') contributions to the social welfare fund
2 lower contributions will help my company's finances
3 paying lower employee's contributions myself should mean I'll be better off
4 I'd better listen for details of how much money is involved
5 this speaker must be an opposition MP
6 he sounds Welsh
7 he's making a good point
8 we might be able to afford that car now.

In short, active listening involves much more than just recognizing what is being said—although even that can be difficult in some circumstances, such as over a poor telephone line or when listening to an unfamiliar accent. Comprehension is multi-layered, requiring (or allowing) interpretation at different levels. When we listen in our own language, we 'go beyond' the *input* in all sorts of ways.

This is something that language learners may need help with: some researchers have found that lower-level learners tend not to use the effective listening strategies that they would apply in their first language. This is a point I will pick up again in Chapters 2 and 5.

## Comprehension and foreign language development

I said earlier that what matters about simplification is *whether or not it works* for the person it is intended for. For language learners, successful comprehension has an importance beyond the short-term satisfaction of having understood. Comprehension is now regarded as an important potential route to progress in the foreign language. There are some applied linguists who regard it as the primary route; probably the best known is Steven Krashen. He has formulated a number of hypotheses about foreign language learning, but for our purposes the central one is the Input Hypothesis. (*How Languages Are Learned* by Patsy Lightbown and Nina Spada (1993) contains—among much else—an excellent summary of Krashen's writings.)

The Input Hypothesis claims that the mental mechanisms of language learning are driven mainly by the learner's experience of *comprehensible input*, that is, messages expressed at an appropriate level of linguistic complexity and in a helpful context. According to Krashen, we make progress in the language by understanding messages expressed in a way that is slightly beyond our current level of competence, but which we can make sense of by using background knowledge and the context.

Although Krashen has modified his original hypotheses in various ways, he has kept to his belief that under suitable *affective* conditions (positive feelings and motivation), language learners will use some parts of this input not only to comprehend the current message, but also to pick up (Krashen's term is *acquire*) new items of grammar and vocabulary and to improve their fluency in speaking.

This makes it especially important that we give learners the chance to practise ways of 'managing' conversations, i.e. getting their partner to slow down, to clarify obscure meanings, to repeat, and so on.

Krashen's claims have sparked a great deal of controversy, in relation to both the background theory and classroom practice. On the theoretical level, many writers have attacked the distinction Krashen makes between 'acquisition' and 'learning'; he argues that the processes by which learners 'acquire' a foreign language (unconsciously, in informal situations and in freer conversation-type tasks) and those by which they 'learn' it (paying conscious attention to language, such as in some form-focused classroom activities) are entirely separate. This issue is one I will be coming back to in Chapter 2.

Among the practical questions arising from the Input Hypothesis are: What are the essential features of comprehensible input? Which parts of the input become available? What are the right conditions for making progress in the foreign language? Krashen has been criticized on a number of grounds, in particular for not producing enough evidence to support his claims. I will illustrate the debate by mentioning just one criticism. Lydia White has objected that access to 'simplified input' would provide learners with impoverished language data: 'by talking to learners only in simple sentences one is depriving them of input which is crucial' (White 1987: 102). Krashen might well say that White is using the term 'simplified input' in the narrow sense of language modified only in terms of its form—pronunciation, grammar, and vocabulary. As I will show in Chapters 3 and 4, one of the lessons from research into native–non-native conversation is that the modifications that enhance learners' comprehension most are those the native speaker makes to the *interaction* (the overall participation patterns) rather than any adjustments to the forms of language used.

In spite of the criticisms of the Input Hypothesis, what is not in dispute is that comprehension plays a vital role in learners' progress. We could hardly expect their language competence to improve without under-standing—except in those strictly limited cases where rote learning might help. But it is now generally accepted that access to comprehensible input is not by itself sufficient. In Chapter 4 I will be summarizing some of the evidence that one of the more effective routes by which new language items are acquired is through interactive negotiation.

# Summary

Conversation is a collaborative enterprise and makes demands on both (or all) the partners. Negotiation and repair play a part in all interaction and are not unique forms of language behaviour involving non-native speak-ers. However, negotiation takes on a special value in the language class-room, since some of the input made comprehensible through interaction may be absorbed into the learners' expanding language knowledge. In this sense, simplification—that is, *successful* simplification—contributes both to the current communicative event and to longer-term language devel-opment.

These complementary aspects of the foreign language classroom experi-ence—input-for-comprehension and input-for-learning—can be expressed in two phrasal verbs: 'getting through' and 'getting on'. In the short term, one can talk about the act of communication as 'getting through to some-one', or 'getting the message through'; a teacher might even talk, less ambi-tiously, about simply 'getting through a lesson'. On the other hand, one talks about students' overall progress in terms of their 'getting on'.

In the rest of this book my aim will be to suggest ways in which teach-ers can usefully highlight particular aspects of the natural process of com-munication in the language classroom. Among the things we will be looking at are:

- how to create tasks that will make it likely that learners will need to negotiate meaning
- how to draw learners' attention to particular aspects of the process of negotiation
- how to respond to their performance in the classroom.

In short, I hope to show how we can help learners to get through *and* get on.

## Suggestions for further reading

*Communication*
**Cook, G.** 1989. *Discourse.* Oxford: Oxford University Press. A good introduction to discourse analysis (the study of speech and writing in context), with plenty of examples from language teaching materials.

*Classroom communication*
**Sinclair, J.** and **M. Coulthard.** 1975. *Towards an Analysis of Discourse.* Oxford: Oxford University Press. This is one of the best-known books on how teachers talk in lessons, based on the authors' research in primary and secondary schools in Britain. Not specific to language teaching.

*Foreign language communication*
**Long, M.** 1983. 'Linguistic and conversational adjustments to non-native speakers.' *Studies in Second Language Acquisition* 5/2: 177–93.

**Varonis, E.** and **S. Gass.** 1985. 'Non-native/non-native conversation: a model for the negotiation of meaning.' *Applied Linguistics* 6/1: 71–90.

These two journal articles complement each other. Michael Long describes the ways in which native speakers try to prevent or resolve problems of communication with a non-native speaker. Evangeline Varonis and Susan Gass show that, when both partners are non-native speakers, the ways in which they deal with problems are similar to those used by native speakers.

*Comprehension and learning*
**Krashen, S.** 1985. *The Input Hypothesis: Issues and Implications.* London: Longman. This book offers a convenient summary of Steven Krashen's theories of language learning. He deals in particular with input obtained through reading, although his views on the role of input apply to listening too.

**Lightbown, P.** and **N. Spada.** 1993. *How Languages are Learned.* Oxford: Oxford University Press. An excellent book, providing a clear summary of a variety of theory-based approaches to language learning. The authors discuss research studies and use extracts from language lessons to show that even the most 'practical' of classroom tasks reflects some theory.

*Repair*
**Schegloff, E., G. Jefferson,** and **H. Sacks.** 1977. 'The preference for self-correction in the organization of repair in conversation.' *Language* 53: 361–82.

**Schwartz, J.** 1980. 'The negotiation of meaning: repair in conversations between second language learners of English' in D.Larsen-Freeman (ed.): *Discourse in Second Language Research.* Rowley, Mass.: Newbury House. pp. 138–53.

Again, you could think of these two as a complementary pair. The article by Emmanuel Schegloff and colleagues has been very influential in showing that native speakers of English tend to repair problems in ways that avoid direct correction. Joan Schwartz applied the same analysis and found that non-native speakers of English also showed a tendency to avoid conflict.

# 2 SIMPLICITY AND ACCESSIBILITY

My account of a listener's interpretation of a speech in the budget debate in Chapter 1 (page 13) suggests that comprehension is both complex and highly individual. Although we often talk of 'sharing' a language with others, it would be wrong to think of a language community as a single cultural group. Each of us belongs to a number of sub-cultures defined by education, employment, social class, religion, leisure interests, region, sex, age, and so on. Differences in the values and beliefs of different cultural groups, and in the knowledge that their members are assumed to possess, can make comprehension difficult even in our own language.

## *Activity*

### Beyond the text

For the three real-life examples below I have provided you with a minimum of background information: time, place, and whether the text was spoken or written. As you read them, see what additional information 'beyond the text' you find yourself using, or seeking, in trying to understand them. What was the writer or speaker referring to? In what situation was the text produced?

*Example 2.1*
> While widows are now usually accepted, orphans are considered unsightly and should be avoided whenever possible.
> (written text, USA, 1985)

*Example 2.2*
> The sangat having langar at Chandigarh's Sector 19-D gurdwara on Monday.
> (written text, India, 1993)

*Example 2.3*
> it's rather an odd offside field for a night-watchman + just two slips + + third man cover and longish mid-off
> (spoken text, England, 1994)

# Comprehension resources

In working out what information you needed in order to make those meanings clearer, you probably used any or all of three types of information: your knowledge of English, the context, and background knowledge. I chose those three examples on the assumption that they would puzzle you. By limiting your access to the context and not revealing their *co-text* (in other words, the text that preceded and followed them), I hoped to force you to use your own internal resources in trying to work out the topic. Of course, it may be that you immediately recognized where the texts were from and what they were about. So if you correctly identified them as an extract from a word processing manual (Example 2.1), a caption under a photograph of a Sikh celebration (Example 2.2), and a snippet from a cricket commentary (Example 2.3), then your life experiences must be sufficiently like mine for you to make sense of the three texts.

I can summarize the relationship between the three principal resources that we use in understanding texts in this way:

Background knowledge

+

Context                    = COMPREHENSION

+

Language

*Figure 2.1: Information sources in comprehension* (adapted from Anderson and Lynch 1988: 13)

Background knowledge—the top level—covers a wide range of information and experience stored in memory: for example, general knowledge of scientific facts and historical events, the beliefs and conventions of our culture; local knowledge about the place we live, and the individual experiences of our social and private lives. At the bottom of the diagram is our knowledge of language, which has been either picked up informally, in the case of the mother tongue, or learnt through formal teaching, in the case of a foreign language.

Linking the top and bottom levels is the context in which we see or hear the text. This is a powerful resource for comprehension and helps us to narrow down the possible meanings of words like 'iron', for example, which can have a dozen or more dictionary meanings. Context is something that we may be more aware of it when it is not there (as in Examples 2.1 to 2.3) than when it is.

Researchers sometimes use the term *bottom-up* and *top-down* to refer to the routes we take to comprehension. In the purest form of bottom-up processing, the listener or reader would first recognize the smallest bits of information in the text (sounds or letters) and then build them up into words, into phrases, into clauses, and so on, until the whole text had been decoded. Taking this route to comprehension is uncommon, although there certainly are situations in which we may be conscious of adopting this bit-by-bit process. If you have tried to decipher barely legible handwriting, or make out the details on a faint photocopy, or to read a street name in a country where you do not know the script well, then you will probably recall what it was like to have to deal with these basic problems of text. But these situations are relatively unusual; you may have noticed that the verbs I used (decode, decipher, make out) are not the ones we generally use to describe comprehension.

On the other hand, in some situations the topic or the speaker is so familiar that we can take for granted a great deal of what is said. We do not need to pay much attention to the language used. This is known as *top-down processing*: comprehension driven by our expectations, based on top-level background knowledge. Top-down processing allows us to anchor our comprehension on what we think is relevant knowledge of the topic, the speaker, and so on. The context provides additional guidance as to what the speaker or writer may wish to tell us, and the linguistic forms used are relatively unimportant.

There is a third route to comprehension—or rather a combination of the first two. We understand by integrating top and bottom information, shuttling between the different sources of knowledge as we pick up clues in the text, and gradually clarifying our understanding of the message. One term for this use of different information sources in parallel is *interactive processing.* When dealing with messages in our own language, this is the form of comprehension we use most often. In unusual situations, such as poor acoustic conditions, or dealing with an unfamiliar accent or difficult terminology, we may be obliged to pay greater attention to bottom-level information.

One way of thinking about comprehension is to use the analogy of a 'do-it-yourself' furniture construction kit—an idea suggested by Christine Nuttall. A novice at furniture building has to follow the written instructions step by step, and may need to re-read certain parts of the text in order to sort out what it means. A more experienced person may be able to dispense with the instructions altogether, or read carefully only at particular points. This analogy is useful because it emphasizes that, in a way, we have to 'assemble' meaning from what the speaker or author offers us. The implication of interactive processing for the foreign language classroom is that teachers can take active steps to make a message accessible by providing assistance at any or all of the three levels—language, context, or background knowledge. In Chapters 3 and 4 I will be looking at various ways in which teachers modify two complementary aspects of classroom language—linguistic input and conversational interaction—in order to make the message understood. But before considering the language *modifications* that teachers make, I turn in the next section to the non-linguistic factors that can be exploited in making meanings accessible in more general terms.

# Non-linguistic simplification

## Context

In face-to-face conversation the immediate physical context provides information about *who, what, when, where,* and so on. In other circumstances, such as listening to the radio, we are deprived of this sort of help. So radio texts often include more explicit references to context than would be found in, say, their television equivalents; in this way they compensate for the absence of visual information. Example 2.4 is part of a transcript of an interview with a dentist (D) for a radio programme, on the topic of new materials that might replace the conventional amalgam used in dental fillings. I have underlined the parts of the interview where the reporter (R) provides the audience with additional information about context.

*Example 2.4*

    D  the other difficulty with them is that in order to get the correct
        occlusal or surface contour we have to once they're set grind them

down with a burr + which does + can take a little time and is also fairly difficult to do by comparison with our conventional materials

R   well there is another alternative and that's the use of what are called glass ionymer cements + now what sort of materials are these?

D   they come usually as a powder and a liquid + and you actually get a small chemical reaction going on + + this + we can now do in a mixing capsule which you put into a mixing machine which is vibrated

R   <u>yes you've actually got one of these here</u>

D   that's right

R   <u>and the powder is what + inside this inside this tube</u>

D   that's right

R   so how do you get it out? + you take the + +

D   what happens is that you put the + + actually activate it by pressing the top and the liquid is released into the capsule + + this is then vibrated

R   <u>oh so now you just squeeze the top of</u>

D   that's right

R   <u>that capsule down</u>

D   we put it into there and you can hear the click
*(click)*

R   <u>oh 'click' yes</u>

D   that's

R   <u>and now the liquid is being released into the + oh yes I can see it coming down the side + mixing with powder</u>

D   that's right + it then goes into a mechanical vibrator *(noise)* and then once that's done we break the capsule open + and you have a + cylinder of material which we can manipulate

R   <u>and then so you + take it out and you manipulate it</u>

D   again we can pick it up + it's rather like slicing through a piece of cheese + we lift a piece up + on a + + fla- what we call a flat plastic + and deposit it in the cavity + + it can then be condensed in the same way as we do conventional filling material + + and you + tamp it into the bottom of the cavity *(noise)*

(*Medicine Now*, BBC Radio 4: 3 August 1994)

In that extract we can see the points at which the reporter felt he had to make explicit the actions that he could see happening in front of him. In effect he added a running commentary on the dentist's demonstration of how to make the new cement. This additional communicative work is part and parcel of working in radio: to make the message as user-friendly as the medium requires. This example is fairly typical of the way the listener is compensated for the lack of access to the visual context.

Example 2.4 also shows that the specialist D was aware of the need to make the message accessible to the audience. But the help he gave the listeners was rather different. While the reporter R offered additional contextual information, what D did was to add explanations of the language, of the sort we saw in the case of 'procurator fiscal' (Example 1.6). Here, speaker D clarified three terms he thought might be unfamiliar to the non-specialist listeners: 'occlusal', 'flat plastic', and—later in the interview—'cariestatic'.

1  in order to get the correct occlusal <u>or surface</u> contour
2  we lift a piece up on a fla- <u>what we call a flat plastic</u>
3  there's a lot of work which has demonstrated that these materials appear to be cariestatic + <u>they reduce the risk of people getting recurrent cari- + + decay + in their teeth</u>.

So in Example 2.4 we can see two speakers contributing in different ways to the process of simplifying a message for the unseen audience: speaker R describes the accompanying actions in order to give listeners additional information about the immediate context, while speaker D provides alternative expressions for unfamiliar terms in an effort to make the language clearer.

This has three implications for the language classroom. The first is that teachers need to be aware that listening materials based on off-air recordings are likely to contain more explicit language than in tapes of face-to-face conversations, even if the programmes feature spontaneous talk (such as the interview in Example 2.4). The second is that when teaching reading or listening we can help our students to make the text more understandable by providing more context and not just by explaining particular language items. The third lesson to draw from the radio interview is that native listeners, too, need help in making sense of what they can hear but not see.

## Background knowledge

We saw that speaker D assumed that his listeners would be familiar with the *concept* of tooth decay, but not with the technical term for it, *caries*. However, in many cases it is our unfamiliarity with the appropriate background knowledge that prevents us understanding something, rather than inadequate knowledge of the language or context.

## Activity

The two examples below are transcripts of reports on the same event, covered by different BBC1 television news programmes on the same day in 1985. Most people find one of the reports simpler than the other. Do you? If so, which one and why?

*Example 2.5*

> The film *Amadeus*, about Mozart, picked up eight Oscars at last night's award ceremony. The award for Best Supporting Actress went to Dame Peggy Ashcroft in *A Passage to India*. She has got flu and did not collect it herself but is said to be delighted. She was also to have been present at the funeral today of Sir Michael Redgrave. He was buried this morning. His three children were there, and many other acting friends.

*Example 2.6*

> The film world's most famous awards, the Oscars, were announced in Hollywood last night, with the usual mix of surprises and disappointments. British films did not do as well as was hoped, although there was one top award for a British star. Most of the Oscars went to the American film *Amadeus*. This is a story about the composer Mozart and won eight Oscars, including Best Film of the Year. Some people had been waiting three days for a glimpse of the celebrities arriving for the ceremony. The American pop star Prince was among them, dressed in purple. But one of the top awards did go to a British star. Dame Peggy Ashcroft won her first Oscar at the age of 77, for Best Supporting Actress in the film *A Passage to India*.

Seen from the point of view of the language used in the two passages, text 2.5 is simpler. It contains fewer sentences (six, compared with eight) and those sentences are shorter (roughly 13 words on average, against 16 in text 2.6). Also the sentences in 2.5 are less complex; only one has more than one verb, and that features co-ordination (with 'and' and 'but') rather than the subordination found in the longest sentence in 2.6. So there are a number of reasons for regarding the second news item as more difficult than the first.

On the other hand, when we consider the information content of the two passages, a rather different picture emerges. In particular, if we think about the *assumed knowledge* required to interpret the message, we can see that the scriptwriter of text 2.5 expects viewers already to possess a certain amount of topical knowledge, while the writer of text 2.6 fills in relatively more background. Compare the ways in which the 'same' information is presented in the news items:

(2.5) The film *Amadeus* about Mozart

(2.6) . . . the <u>American</u> film *Amadeus*. This is a story about <u>the composer</u> Mozart . . .

(2.5) (eight) Oscars

(2.6) <u>the film world's most famous awards</u>, the Oscars

These differences could simply be due to personal style or to time constraints, but they may stem from the fact that the scripts were written for two different audiences. Example 2.5 came from *The Six O'Clock News*, an early evening bulletin broadcast for a general audience; Example 2.6 was transmitted an hour or so earlier in *John Craven's Newsround*, a children's news programme. The fact that 2.6 was for a younger audience would help to explain why the film clip included a shot of a pop star arriving for the ceremony. The relationship between the two news items is similar to that between the two forms of simplification—restrictive and elaborative—which I discussed in Chapter 1. The adult item is relatively simple in linguistic terms, but assumes much more background knowledge; the children's version is linguistically more complex but cognitively more accessible, since it fills in the factual details that the writer believes are unfamiliar to the audience.

## Simple = accessible?

The six examples show that the more we know, the less we need to rely on language to understand the message. Conversation between friends or colleagues can be almost incomprehensible to outsiders, or rather outsiders may understand what is being said at a superficial level, but not what is being referred to or implied. Below is a brief exchange of comments from a conversation which I overheard some years ago. The details of the context were these:

*Scene:*    a train from London to Edinburgh, approaching Berwick station on the English–Scottish border
*Time:*    late December 1984 (between Christmas and New Year—a time when many British people travel to see members of their family)
*Speakers:* two elderly women (possibly sisters)

As we pulled into Berwick station, one of the women, J, looked through the window and then spoke to K, who was gathering her belongings together:

*Example 2.7*
    J    ah I can see David + + ALONE
    K    oh? *(high-rise intonation, showing surprise)*
    J    MUCH better
    K    hm *(high-fall, suggesting agreement?)*

At this point I would like to pause and ask you to reflect on the way you have interpreted the exchange between the two women. You and I cannot know precisely what lay behind their words—and as overhearers we have no right to—but we may hazard a guess. We know that J had expected to be met at the station by someone called David, who was likely to be accompanied by at least one other person. But what do we make of J's comment 'much better' and K's 'hm'? It could mean that David was looking much better—in terms of his state of health or general appearance—than he had done the last time they saw him. It could be that what was 'better' was simply the fact that he was alone.

When we try to make sense of other people's conversations, we can use the conventional meaning of the words uttered and perhaps additional information from the context, to reach some sort of understanding. But we can never be sure of recovering the real original meaning, the unspoken part of what they said. Language used for a particular purpose in a particular context takes on a particular meaning for the audience it is intended for; this is called *pragmatic meaning*. Interpreting pragmatic meaning involves working out the assumptions behind what is said and the effect the person intended their message to achieve. In Example 2.7, why did J tell K that David was alone? She was not simply informing her; K would soon have discovered for herself that David was unaccompanied.

From what they said and the way that they said it, I understood what they meant to be something like this:

J    I can see David but (X) isn't with him.

K    Oh? I wonder why (he/she) hasn't come along too?

J    Actually it's much better that (he/she) isn't with David because it means we can talk more freely about (. . .)

K    I agree.

I may be wrong, of course. My understanding of the exchange depends on an assumption that J and K disapproved of David's wife or partner. Other interpretations are possible. For example, it could be that David had a large and boisterous dog, which the two women disliked. Or that they were glad that he was alone (i.e. that there was nobody else on the station platform) because they were usually embarrassed by what they felt were David's over-affectionate greetings.

It would round off the story nicely if I were now able to reveal what the two women actually meant. But since this was a private conversation, I was obviously unable to ask J and K for confirmation that I had understood them correctly. I was, after all, listening in to *their* conversation.

Although the specific details of Example 2.7 may be trivial, it illustrates an important point: that the relationship between simple language and accessible meaning is not straightforward. Extremely basic language can express, or hint at, highly complex messages. A vital part of being an effective listener/reader involves 'going beyond the text', using the clues and hints to recover the speaker's/writer's intended meaning. A great deal of research has now been carried out into the influence of various sources of information (topic knowledge, access to context and co-text, language cues) on foreign language comprehension. The current view is that, provided learners have reached a certain threshold proficiency level, unfamiliarity of topic and text structure is likely to hamper comprehension more than linguistic difficulty itself (Johnson 1981, 1982, Carrell 1987). The other side of the coin is that, although teachers should of course help learners to cope with the linguistic difficulties of a text, we should also encourage them to use contextual cues and background knowledge to increase their understanding. I will be returning to this issue at various points in the book.

# Simplifying texts

One way to make a message more accessible—as we saw in the case of the 'Oscar' texts—is to make it richer in information, which will tend to make it linguistically more complex. The other is to make it linguistically simpler, although this can be problematic, as John Honeyfield has shown. There is a risk that simplified reading texts will be made unnaturally and unhelpfully plain, so to speak. In an unsimplified text the important information is distributed unevenly through the text, with occasional peaks of key information—'relatively isolated, relatively unpredictable items requiring high points in the reader's attention' (Honeyfield 1977: 434). Learning to read a foreign language well requires us to get used to spotting the clues in texts that indicate where those peaks are. One of the effects of simplifying the language of a text can be to flatten out the textual landscape. Honeyfield illustrates the problem with a paragraph from a simplified reader based on Thor Heyerdahl's *The Kon-Tiki Expedition*:

*Example 2.8*

> We were rather worried about the ropes. We did not think about them during the day. We were too busy. But we thought about them during the night. We lay on mats in the cabin. Then we could feel and hear the ropes. The logs moved under us. They were like an animal breathing. The first two nights were the worst. Later the water swelled the ropes. The ropes then held the nine logs together more tightly. But they still moved about.
> (Wymer 1973: 35)

This simplified version feels 'choppy' and staccato, which makes it more difficult for the reader to recognize the relationship between one piece of information and the next. So 'simplifying' the grammar can have disadvantages. There may also be a price to be paid for simplifying the vocabulary of a text to put it within the learner's reach. One of the ironies of

English simplification is that the simpler and more common a word is, the more likely it is to have more than one meaning. The result is that replacing a more difficult or less frequent word with a simpler and more frequent one often increases the difficulty of a text (Davies and Widdowson 1974).

A number of researchers have investigated the effects of various types of textual simplification by comparing the comprehension achieved by learners reading different versions of the same text, but the results are contradictory. Some have found that grammatically simplified material is less well understood than the original. Other studies have found that grammatical simplification does assist learners' comprehension. The differences in results do not seem to be related to students' level in the foreign language.

From a common-sense point of view, syntactic simplification *ought* to work. After all, few teachers would argue against the proposition that students with good knowledge of grammar will encounter fewer problems in an unsimplified text than those with a poorer knowledge. So if a text contains less difficult syntax, one might expect it to be easier for weaker learners to understand than an unsimplified version. Why, then, has some research shown that language learners' comprehension is not assisted by linguistic simplification, and may even be hampered by it? The answer could be that there is bad simplification and good simplification, and that the success of simplification can only be judged by reference to a particular learner or group of learners. This takes us back to the point I made in Chapter 1, that simplification can be used to describe the *action* or the *effect* of simplifying. A 'simplified text' that is not understood is not a simplified text.

A similar point can be made about some of the attempts to create 'simplified' spoken texts for listening courses. Materials especially scripted for language learners often reduce the amount of language available from a speaker in a natural setting and make the listening task unnaturally difficult. For example, one of the variables most frequently used to grade the difficulty of listening materials is the length of the text, the assumption being that learners should encounter shorter texts before longer ones. However, this conflicts with what has been observed to happen in real-life communication between native and non-native speakers. As we will· see in Chapter 3, one way in which native speakers successfully modify their speech to assist a non-native partner is to give them several chances to take in any difficult parts of what they are saying. They encourage their partner to ask for clarification, respond to requests for help, repeat, and so on. The effect of this is that the native speaker produces *more* words than they would to a fellow native speaker. So they take longer to convey the message, but in so doing make it more accessible. I will discuss some of the implications of this for the design of listening tasks in Chapter 5.


# Explanation

We have seen that explanations can take the form of additional information inserted into a text or conversation to explain a concept or to paraphrase an expression. In the section 'Terms for negotiation' in Chapter 1 (page 10), I referred to Craig Chaudron's research into the linguistic behaviour of teachers giving the same lesson to native and non-native listeners (Chaudron 1979). His conclusion was that a learner has to reach a certain level of proficiency to be able to recognize when the teacher is attempting to clarify an unfamiliar word or expression. At elementary levels the learners may assume that the intended elaborations are in fact providing *new* information, rather than paraphrases of what the speaker has just said.

For the classroom this means that, when explaining a problematic item, we need to give our students clear signals that what we are saying is related to what we have just said, and in what way. Unless we provide a clue such as 'in other words' or 'that is', they may not recognize the additional information that could help them understand. Example 2.9 (below) illustrates what can happen if a teacher does not give a clear signal of explanation. It comes from a lesson in which a group of adult lower-intermediate English learners are working on a physical description task. The teaching point is the superlative form of adjectives. The teacher has spread out a number of pictures and photographs of people and has been getting the learners to describe them in various ways.

*Example 2.9*
>      T   who's got the most problems do you think?
>      P   perhaps the + the black woman
>      T   the black woman yeah + she looks the most resigned +
>      P   yes
>      T   doesn't she + I can't do anything about it + + here I am +     5
>          yes she looks the most resigned I think + hm possibly + +
>          she looks fairly ordinary doesn't she
>      Ss  yes
>      T   ordinary + + yeah + that's right ok then + what I want you
>          to do . . .
>      (observation data)

From the way I have represented that short interaction between teacher and students, it is probably unclear that parts of the teacher's third speaking turn (lines 5–7) were intended to explain the word 'resigned'. To help bring out the pragmatic meaning of his words, here is a version with 'stage directions' added:

> T   who's got the most problems do you think?
> P   perhaps the + the black woman
> T   the black woman yeah + she looks the most resigned +
> P   yes
> T   doesn't she + *(changing his voice and accent)* 'I can't do anything about it' + + *(adopting a glum facial expression)* 'here I am' + yes she looks the most resigned I think +  hm possibly + + *(pointing to another photograph)* SHE looks fairly ordinary doesn't she
> Ss  yes
> T   ordinary + + yeah + that's right ok then + what I want you to do . . .

Adding the comments in brackets should make it clearer that the two utterances inside quotation marks ('I can't do anything about it' and 'here I am') were in fact an attempt by the teacher to express the *thoughts* of the woman in the photograph that the students were looking at. He was trying to explain the meaning of the word 'resigned' by reinforcing the image of resignation captured by the camera. Instead of saying something such as 'resigned means you feel you can't change the situation you're in', he chose to explain the word dramatically, using his voice (changing his accent) and his face (pulling the corners of his mouth downwards). But since the students were all looking down at the photograph and not at him, my impression was that his attempted explanation was unsuccessful.

It is possible that the 'yes' from student P might be a signal that she had managed to infer the meaning of 'resigned' from the photograph. However, as P was from Spain, she may have recognized the word from its similarity with the Spanish equivalent *resignada*, so her 'yes' might show agreement with the teacher's description of the woman in the photograph. A third possibility is that P did not actually understand the word at all, but having heard a positive comment ('she looks . . .') followed by 'hm?' with rising intonation, she realized that the teacher was trying to elicit a 'yes'—so she gave him what he wanted.

A similar problem arises when we try to interpret the chorus of 'yes' produced by the students after the teacher's third turn.

> T   . . . yes she looks the most resigned I think + hm possibly + + she looks fairly ordinary doesn't she
> Ss  yes

The fact that a number of the students said 'yes' after the teacher's 'doesn't she?' does not mean that we can be sure what they were saying 'yes' to. Represented as they are in the first version, it looks as if the teacher's two utterances 'she looks the most resigned I think' and 'she looks fairly ordinary doesn't she?' implied that 'ordinary' is an alternative expression for 'resigned'. After all, from the learners' point of view it could be as 'logical' to assume that the second utterance is an elaboration of the first, as it was for the teacher to think the learners should recognize the link between 'Here I am' with 'I can't do anything about it'.

In fact, as I have shown in the second version of the transcript, the teacher had turned his attention to another photograph. He probably felt he had made clear to the class that he had finished with his teaching point about 'resigned'. By pausing after 'possibly' and pointing to another photograph and pronouncing 'SHE' with contrastive stress, he expected the students to understand that he was now introducing a new adjective, 'ordinary', to refer to a different woman. However, when we bear in mind the post-elementary level of these learners, it seems doubtful that they would have picked up the pausing and stress clues that the teacher offered.

I have discussed this short extract in some detail to make the point that, from the learner's point of view, the classroom can be a confusing place. 'Explanations' are only explanations if they are recognized. One researcher who has consistently tried to view classroom interaction from the learner's perspective is Dick Allwright. In particular, he stresses that what a teacher thinks of as 'explanations' or 'corrections' or 'prompts' are not necessarily clear and unambiguous acts. Learners have to *interpret* teachers' intentions, not just recognize them. Allwright pithily sums up the problems that learners face in trying to make sense of what the teacher is doing: 'the only thing that saves learners from utter confusion in class is their relative lack of attention to the potentially confusing features of classroom interaction' (Allwright 1984: 217).

## Accessible versus noticeable

So far I have looked at three main areas in which a speaker or writer can make a text more accessible:

– linguistic simplification
– contextual information
– relevant background.

In one-way communication such as reading or listening to the radio, individuals have to make use of these cues themselves (if they can) in order to understand the text better. In two-way communication the learner can ask for explanation and negotiate meaning with the other speaker.

The practical lesson for language teachers is not that we should not elaborate, but that we need to give our students clear signals as to when we are doing it and which item we want to clarify. This brings us to an important distinction, between what is *accessible* and what is *noticeable*. Our task as teachers is more than merely to make input comprehensible and to foster communication in the short term—important though those things are. We are there to teach or, to use the current term, to 'facilitate learning'. One of the implications of Krashen's Input Hypothesis (mentioned in Chapter 1) appeared to be that all we needed to do was to ensure that input was comprehensible and leave our students' in-built acquisition mechanism to do the rest.

However, the consensus now is that Krashen overstated the case for comprehensible input. Although it is of course important, comprehensible input is not sufficient by itself to result in acquisition, or rather to result in progress at the sort of rate one would expect to achieve in formal learning conditions. One of those who argued that the Input Hypothesis provides only a partial explanation of language learning is Merrill Swain. She based her argument on an analysis of the performance in French of English-speaking learners in Canada. These learners attended an immersion programme at secondary school, in which they studied all subjects through French. Despite seven years' exposure to comprehensible input (i.e. meaningful academic content, modified to their receptive level), the learners' performance on tests was considerably below that of native speakers. Although they had achieved fluency in spoken French, they did rather poorly in specific areas such as writing and grammatical knowledge.

Why was their performance limited in this way? Swain's explanation is that their French was limited not by lack of exposure to input but by lack of a need to *produce* accurate French. Throughout the immersion period these learners were using French to communicate with fellow English-speakers (learners and teachers), so they were able to 'get through' by using language that was inaccurate, but adequate for communication. The outcome of Swain's research was the *Comprehensible Output Hypothesis*: this says that meaningful communication in the language classroom 'needs to incorporate the notion of being pushed toward the delivery of a message that is not only conveyed, but that is conveyed precisely, coherently and appropriately' (Swain 1985: 248–9).

The hypothesis rests on four assumptions:

– that learners learn to speak by speaking

- that they need to be 'pushed' to use alternative means of expression when communication breaks down
- that using the foreign language offers them the chance to try out new forms and expressions
- that being 'pushed' in performance shifts their attention from meaning to form.

A number of other researchers have tested the Comprehensible Output Hypothesis and in general the evidence suggests that learners *can* be pushed to a higher level of accuracy by the natural requirement to negotiate meaning when a communication problem arises. I will be commenting further on three of these research studies in Chapter 4.

Swain's work suggests that, as well as setting learners communicative tasks, we need to find ways of drawing attention to the forms of language used (or not used) in performing them. In other words, as well as ensuring that they gain experience of making messages accessible, the teacher has to make language items *noticeable*. I am taking this term from the work of Richard Schmidt, who has argued that conscious attention to the form and/or meaning of an item is necessary if the learner is to *notice the gap* between their performance and that of a native speaker. There are close parallels between Schmidt's notion of *noticing* and others such as 'consciousness-raising' (Sharwood Smith 1981).

Schmidt's work is important in reminding us that for classroom activities to be minimally effective as *learning* events (and not just as *practice* of what is already familiar), teachers have to create conditions in which input and output are both accessible and noticeable. This is easier said than done, because not all the students in a class will have precisely the same level, even if they have a common first language and are at the same age. At times the item that the teacher chooses to focus on may be one that is already familiar to one learner but completely new to another.

It is also difficult for teachers to know whether in any specific instance we are helping an individual learner to notice something for the first time, or to notice again something they have encountered but forgotten—and even whether they are noticing it at the moment. We have an example of this in the extract below, which comes from a general English class at pre-intermediate level. As we join them, the class is working in pairs and the teacher has just asked one pair (learner K and his partner) how they are getting on.

*Example 2.10*
> T   are you comparing the agency + the tour agent + or are you comparing the actual tours?
> K   um actual tour

> T   well + + the actual tours?
> K   for this one
> T   uhuh
> K   is Sun Tan Tours + has many tours + + +
> T   hmhm + + yeah try and
> K   tour location + location
> T   you mean many offices + or do you mean many stopovers + or do you mean many destinations?
> K   ah yes <u>destinations</u>
> T   'destinations' that's the word you wanted + has got more destinations + ok

(observation data)

The effect of this brief exchange is to highlight the appropriate word. At least in the short term, K notices the gap between his attempts to express what he wants to say ('actual tour, tour location, location') and the teacher's 'destination'. But is K noticing the word for the first time? Apparently not. Three pieces of evidence suggest that he recognizes the word from some earlier encounter: (1) he is able to repeat it accurately on first hearing, (2) he does not ask for repetition or for spelling, and (3) his 'ah yes'. So what the teacher appears to have done here is to reactivate an item that was already to some degree within K's English repertoire.

What about K's silent partner? Since she said nothing during this exchange between the teacher and K, we (and the teacher) have no way of knowing. Even if she did notice the word 'destination', she may have decided it was not one she needed to add to her stock of words.

This extract and Example 2.9, featuring the word 'resigned', show how difficult it can be to follow what people say *and mean* in the classroom, even when you have the luxury of time to watch a video-recording, as I had in this case. To interpret classroom interaction as it is in progress, as teacher and learners have to do, is much more complicated. In particular it may be hard for learners busy doing communicative tasks to notice the points the teacher wants them to focus on. A number of research studies have shown that what learners actually notice in the classroom—either because of, or in spite of, the teacher's actions—is highly idiosyncratic. When Assia Slimani asked a group of Algerian EFL learners what they had learnt from a sequence of lessons, she found that only three per cent of the items they mentioned in their reports were noticed by most of the class (i.e. three-quarters of the students). Nearly 40 per cent of the items noticed were reported by only one person. More striking still, some 11 per cent of the items that the students said they had learnt in the lessons had not actually occurred in the interaction at all (Slimani 1992).

# Summary

Whatever teachers do to ensure that messages are accessible, final control over what learners actually notice (and may subsequently learn) rests with the learners themselves. As teachers we can do our best to ensure that item X is *noticeable*, but we cannot guarantee that it will be *noticed*—still less, that it will be learnt. The good news is that, meanwhile, learners will probably be busy learning other things that they notice for themselves, without our focusing on them. However, we should not assume that, since learners are likely to notice things other than those their teachers focus on, we need not attempt to draw attention to items we believe are useful. In Chapter 3 I will look at 'Teacher Talk' in detail and then in Chapter 4 will I discuss the evidence from research into what makes new language items accessible and noticeable.

## *Suggestions for further reading*

### *Comprehension processes*
**Anderson, A.** and **T. Lynch.** 1988. *Listening.* Oxford: Oxford University Press. In this book, Anne Anderson and I highlight the active involvement of the listener in the process of understanding and discuss how to bring that into classroom listening tasks.

### *Simplification*
**Davies, A.** 1984. 'Simple, simplified and simplification: what is authentic?' in J. C. Alderson and A. H. Urquhart (eds.): *Reading in a Foreign Language.* London: Longman. pp. 181–98.

**Honeyfield, J.** 1977. 'Simplification.' *TESOL Quarterly* 11/4: 431–40. Both Alan Davies and John Honeyfield discuss the problem of how to facilitate learners' understanding of reading texts, without 'simplifying' the texts so much that they become unnatural (and perhaps more difficult).

*Noticing*

**Schmidt, R.** 1990. 'The role of consciousness in second language learning.' *Applied Linguistics* 11/2: 129–58. In this article, Richard Schmidt explains how 'noticing the gap' is essential to successful learning of a foreign language.

**Slimani, A.** 1992. 'Evaluation of classroom interaction' in J. C. Alderson and A. Beretta (eds.): *Evaluating Second Language Education*. Cambridge: Cambridge University Press. pp. 197–220. Assia Slimani's article is a fascinating account of the differences in what individuals in a language class 'noticed' in a series of language lessons, and of the differences between those perceptions and the teaching points the teacher was working on.

# 3 TEACHER TALK

There are at least three main reasons for the growing interest in the way teachers talk to language learners. The first is that people have recognized the vital link between comprehension and progress in the foreign language. The second is that studies of classroom language have shown that certain aspects of teacher talk, such as the way we ask questions, influence the way learners use the language. The third is the realization that it is not easy for the learners to understand what the teacher is currently trying to focus their attention on. Each of these three reasons relates to a different role played by the teacher: as provider of input, as facilitator of communication, and as instructor.

All this makes it important to think about the options we have for modifying what we say in order to make ourselves understood. In this chapter I will be describing three areas of *modification* in teacher-to-learner language: input, interaction, and information choice.

## Activity

### The hat seller

The six pictures in Figure 3.1 show the story of a hat seller's struggle to outwit a troop of monkeys. I would like you to look through them and pay particular attention to the ending of the story.

Imagine you have decided to tell that story to a class of post-elementary learners. They will listen with a jumbled set of pictures in front of them, which they have to number in the order of appearance in your story. Look through the pictures again and see whether any of the vocabulary that you would use to refer to objects or actions in the story—e.g. 'fist' or 'scratch'— would be hard for post-elementary learners to understand. If so, how would you modify them to make the story accessible to your students?

If possible, show the pictures to one or two colleagues and ask them at which points they think they would make modifications. In particular,

*Figure 3.1: The hat seller and the monkeys* (from Heaton 1966)

ask them how they would tell the last part of the story (pictures 5 and 6). Do you and your colleagues agree on what might be difficult for your students? Are there differences in the way you would express the ending?

At various points in this chapter I will be discussing ways in which a number of native-speaker teachers modified the story when talking to learners of English.

# Input modifications

Early research into native–non-native communication focused on input, in the sense of the forms of language addressed to the non-native listener, and was strongly influenced by the notion of *Foreigner Talk*. This was a term invented by Charles Ferguson, who claimed that people used a special variety of simplified speech when talking to outsiders who they thought had little or no knowledge of the language (Ferguson 1971). The main features of Foreigner Talk were modifications to grammar, vocabulary, and pronunciation.

In the popular stereotype of Foreigner Talk, the native speaker's language is modified to the point where it becomes ungrammatical. In Ferguson's example 'He live three year Japan', the simplification involves leaving out the past tense, the plural endings, and the preposition. I think it may be this stereotypical image of Foreigner Talk that leads some teachers to deny, as I mentioned in Chapter 1, that they use Teacher Talk in the classroom. So it is important to stress that in the large number of studies of language teachers' speech to students, instances of ungrammatical teacher-to-learner talk are actually very rare.

It is true that in non-classroom settings—at work or in government offices, for example—native speakers do produce ungrammatical modifications. However, in a survey of nearly 40 studies of native–non-native conversations outside and inside the classroom, Michael Long found that only one of the classroom studies had revealed ungrammatical speech (Long 1981).

Since Long's survey, there has been a great deal of further research into Teacher Talk. Craig Chaudron's later analysis of some 20 studies shows that the input modifications in classroom settings are only 'occasionally' ungrammatical (Chaudron 1988). In short, in the vast majority of cases, teachers' modified speech does not stray beyond the grammar of the target language. The list in Table 3.1 shows some of the commonest input modifications in Teacher Talk.

| |
|---|
| **Vocabulary**<br>– use of more common vocabulary<br>– avoidance of idioms<br>– use of nouns rather than pronouns |
| **Grammar**<br>– shorter utterances<br>– less complex utterances<br>– more regular surface structure<br>– increased use of present tense |
| **Pronunciation**<br>– slower speech<br>– clearer articulation<br>– more frequent use of standard forms<br>– less vowel-reduction (use of /«/ in English)<br>– greater stress differentiation<br>– wider pitch range<br>– more pauses<br>– longer pauses |
| **Non-verbal**<br>– increased use of gesture<br>– increased use of facial expression |

*Table 3.1: Input modifications*

As I said in Chapter 1, it is not possible to separate Teacher Talk off from the way language is spoken in other settings. Everything about it is relative; we can only judge how much teachers are modifying their speech by comparing it with the way they would express the same message to native listeners. This is difficult to do in a natural way. There are certainly some real-life circumstances in which such a comparison is possible: for example, I mentioned Chaudron's study of a Canadian lecturer giving parallel versions of the same lecture to native and non-native audiences.

However, language teachers do not typically teach the same lessons to both natives and non-natives, and so it is often hard to make a direct comparison between 'native' and 'non-native' talk. In order to illustrate how teachers adapt their modifications to different levels of listener, I will use extracts from an experiment designed to allow a comparison of the language used by teachers of English talking to listeners at varying levels of comprehension ability (Lynch 1986). It involved 24 native-speaker teachers of English from six countries. The non-native listeners were all taking general English courses at language schools in Edinburgh.

I asked the teachers to tell three stories to four listeners in turn. They told the stories spontaneously (that is, without rehearsal or notes) but based them on sets of pictures like those in the Activity. The listeners had the same set of pictures but in jumbled order; their task was to follow the teacher's story and to number the pictures in the correct order, to match what they heard.

The teachers told the stories first to the native listener and then to the advanced, intermediate, and elementary learners, in that order. Examples 3.1 and 3.2 come from the performance of a female Scottish teacher telling the monkey story. They illustrate the first two forms of input modification listed earlier: the use of more common vocabulary and the avoidance of idioms.

### Example 3.1: Using more common vocabulary
In her introduction to the story, the teacher used these expressions to refer to the hat seller:

> *Native:*        'a weaver'
> *Advanced:*    'a weaver + he used to weave straw hats'
> *Intermediate:* 'a weaver + he made hats and baskets'
> *Elementary:*   'an old man who made hats and sold hats'
> (experimental data)

### Example 3.2: Avoiding idioms
When describing what happened after the hat seller scratched his head in puzzlement, she said:

*Native:*           'the penny dropped'
*Advanced:*         'it dawned on him'
*Intermediate:*     'and then he realized'
*Elementary:*       'he thought + and he realized + + it was easy'
(experimental data)

So this teacher adopted similar strategies in the two situations, to help the two lower-level listeners to understand her story. In her introduction (Example 3.1) she used a relatively uncommon noun, 'weaver', to three of the listeners. For the fellow native listener, she used it without comment. For the advanced and intermediate learners, she used it and then explained it. However, when telling the story to the elementary learner, she replaced it with 'an old man who made hats'. Similarly, in Example 3.2 she used idioms to both native and advanced listeners, but modified for the other two partners by opting for the verb 'realize'—adding 'it was easy' for the elementary-level listener. In both cases, the result of the teacher's input modification was that she produced most words to the weakest listener—an example of the 'elaborative simplification' mentioned in Chapter 1.

It is worth bearing in mind that most research into Teacher Talk has examined lessons where the teacher is a native speaker of the target language or has near-native competence. Lessons given by non-native teachers are likely to contain more instances of ungrammatical language. Some may be intended to help the learners understand what is being said; others may arise as the result of performance slips, or even underlying errors, if the teacher's command of the target language is very limited. But for the purposes of this book, I am concerned only with modifications of speech that stem from a teacher's attempt to make things easier for the learners, and not with deviations due to lack of attention or to inadequacies in language competence.

# Interaction modifications

After the initial interest in Foreigner Talk in the 1970s, researchers shifted their attention from modifications of form to *Foreigner Talk Discourse*, that is, the general patterns of interaction between native and non-native speakers. Looking at the overall picture is important in two ways. Firstly, it takes into account the contributions of both conversation partners. Foreigner Talk was viewed as a language *product*; something produced by the native speaker. The non-native listener played a passive role, as receiver or 'consumer'. On the other hand, the idea of Foreigner Talk Discourse emphasizes the *process* of communication in which both native and non-native speakers play their part.

The second reason why it is important to consider the interaction as a whole is that it is now clear that interaction modifications are *more* influential in assisting learners' comprehension than are modifications of the spoken input alone. In a study comparing the two forms of modification in a listening comprehension task, Teresa Pica and her colleagues at the University of Pennsylvania showed that learners who were allowed to interact with the teacher to clarify a 'difficult' version of a listening text achieved higher scores than those who heard a simplified version but could not interact with her (Pica, Young, and Doughty 1987). I will be discussing this and similar evidence in more detail in the next chapter.

## *Activity*

Examples 3.3 to 3.5 come from recordings of normal classes, in other words, classes not arranged for experimental purposes. They are taken from the opening section of parallel lessons (listening classes based on the same cassette and print material) with three groups of learners on a general English course. The groups were at different levels of proficiency: post-elementary, intermediate, and post-intermediate. In each case the teacher is giving instructions for the listening task.

On the basis of what the teacher says, try to decide which of the groups is post-elementary, intermediate, and post-intermediate.

*Example 3.3*

    T  ok + you'll hear the instructions
    G  we must write anything?
    T  you will hear the instructions on the tape what you have to do yes + you have to + complete + the diagram + in each case + you have + part of a diagram + and you have to complete it according to what the speaker says
    H  excuse me
    T  yes
    H  if any words in speaking I don't understand it can I . . .?
    T  then you say 'stop'
    H  'stop'
    T  ok?
    I  but first we must discuss?
    T  well + no + first you say 'stop'
    I  yes
    T  I will stop the tape and then you discuss what the problem was
    Ss  yeah
    T  maybe it was a problem for one person and not for another and the other person can say what the word was
    H  and if all of us we don't know the . . .

T   right + then you have to decide + what question + you want me + to answer + + it's no good saying 'we want you to help us' + + you have to say exactly what information it is you need

Ss  ok

T   you'll now hear the instructions + which are a shorter version of what I have just said + ok? *(starts the tape)*

## Example 3.4

T   right + do you remember the exercise we did with the + street plans?

Ss  yes

T   where you had to fill in information about shops?

Ss  yes

T   well this is the same kind of thing + this is something + the same idea but this time it's not town plans it's diagrams + but the same principle applies + so what you have to do is you have to listen + to the tape + and you have to decide + 'have we got enough information?' + so + you sort of + discuss this and you say + 'is the information + on the tape enough + for me to + complete the diagram?' + and if it is not enough + you have to ask + questions + to get the information you need + + right? *(starts the tape)*

## Example 3.5

T   right + um + you are going to hear a tape + you have to listen to the tape + and finish + these diagrams + first is this one + and then we'll stop

Ss  yeah

T   at the beginning of the tape + they will tell you what you have to do + + then you will listen to the instructions + for the diagrams + if there's a problem + if you don't understand + you must say + 'stop' + immediately + and I will stop the tape + all right? + so if you hear something + and you don't understand it and you can't do the next thing on here + say 'stop' + + but you can't ask me + + immediately + + to explain + first you have to ask another student

K   uhuh

T   right?

Ss  yeah

T   so you + when somebody says 'stop' + you must talk about the problem

Ss  hm/yeah

T   try to explain it to each other + and really + if you really + can't find the answer + then you can ask me + ok? + but first you must + try to find out from another student + that's important + ok?

**Ss**  ok
**T**  right + all right so first you will do this diagram here + don't worry about these figures + just look at this one + + are you ready?
**L**  excuse me + what we will write here?
**T**  the tape will tell you
**L**  ah
**T**  that's the exercise listening to the tape + + so first you will hear an explanation + you will hear instructions about what you have to do + then you will hear + what you have to do + are you ready?
**Ss**  yes
**T**  *(starts the tape)*
(observational data)

*Solution:* Example 3.3 features the intermediate group, 3.4 the post-intermediate, and 3.5 the post-elementary.

What clues did you use in deciding which group of learners was at which level? You could probably tell by the *input* that the learners in Example 3.4 are more advanced than the other two. For example, the teacher in 3.4 uses the expression 'the same principle applies', which is more difficult than anything in Examples 3.3 or 3.5.

Also, if you look at the general pattern of *interaction*, Example 3.4 looks rather different from 3.3 and 3.5. In 3.4 the teacher gives the task instructions in one main speaking turn. The two contributions from the learners at the start of 3.4 are both in response to the teacher's questions about whether they remember doing a similar listening task. As far as we can tell from the transcript, these learners are having no problem understanding what they hear.

On the other hand, in Examples 3.3 and 3.5 there is much more interaction between teacher and learners (either individually or as a group). In other words, the transcripts show more of the give-and-take of conversation. The way the learners participate in 3.3 and 3.5 shows that they feel a need to get meanings sorted out. Unlike the students in 3.4, they need to take the initiative rather than simply respond to the teacher's checks: they ask for clarification (e.g. 'if any words in speaking I don't understand it can I . . .?' in 3.3, and 'what we will write here?' in 3.5). They get the teacher to confirm that they have interpreted the instructions correctly ('but first we must discuss?' in 3.3).

For their part, too, the teachers contribute to the negotiation of meaning. Both make a point of checking the learners' comprehension, or at least offering them the chance to say they have not understood. In Example

3.3 there are two comprehension checks ('ok?'), and in 3.5 there are six (including 'all right?', 'right?', 'ok?' and 'are you ready?').

The teacher in Example 3.5 increases her chances of being understood by repeating and paraphrasing what she says. She wants to make sure that the procedure for the listening task is absolutely clear before going on, so she explains the basic idea—that if there is a problem, the students are to call 'stop' immediately—in three slightly different ways. In this respect, Example 3.5 reflects a typical pattern of modification to low-proficiency learners: repetition and *reformulation* tend to be most frequent in classrooms where teachers are working with elementary learners.

Examples 3.3 to 3.5 illustrate four of the interaction modifications commonly used by language teachers to increase comprehension: repetition, reformulation, clarification request, and comprehension check. A more complete list is shown in Table 3.2, together with a definition of each from the teacher's point of view.

---

**confirmation check**
making sure that what you have understood is what the learner means

**comprehension check**
making sure that the learner has understood what you mean

**clarification request**
asking the learner to explain or rephrase

**repetition**
repeating your words or those of the learner

**reformulation**
rephrasing the content of what you have said

**completion**
completing the learner's utterance

**backtracking**
returning to a point in the conversation, up to which you believe the learner has understood you

---

*Table 3.2: Interaction modifications*

Although I have discussed input and interaction separately, they are often used in combination, as in Example 3.6. It features a male American teacher telling the monkey story to an elementary-level learner of English.

*Example 3.6*

   S  and he shakes his fist at them + up in the tree
   L  *(frowns)*
   S  he shakes his fist at them
   L  ah ok wait a minute
   S  he waves at them + do you understand?                 5
   L  no
   S  well he wakes up first of all and um + he's angry with the monkeys
   L  ah yeah
   S  because + yes?                                    10
   L  ah yes
   S  because they've taken his hats
   L  yes
   S  and he + shakes his fist that is he waves his arm + at them
   L  hm                                           15
   S  in anger
   L  yes yes
   S  and the monkeys + all wave their arms back at him
   L  yes
   (experimental data)

If we think first in terms of *input* from the teacher, the extract illustrates lexical modification: the teacher twice changes 'shake' to 'wave' (lines 5 and 14), and also replaces 'fist' with 'arm' (line 14). In each case he substitutes a more common word for the less common one he originally chose.

But if we look at the *interaction* adjustments, we get a much richer picture of how the partners collaborate in shaping the progress of their conversation. The learner gives the teacher two signals that he has a comprehension problem. The first is non-verbal: as the teacher says 'he shakes his fist at them + up in the tree', the learner frowns, which leads the teacher to repeat 'he shakes his fist at them'. The learner requests more time to take in the information: 'ah ok wait a minute' (line 4). We then have a sequence in which the teacher uses five types of modification. At line 5 he reformulates the message ('he waves at them'), and then checks the listener's comprehension by explicitly asking 'do you understand?'. When he gets a negative response, he backtracks to an earlier part of the story: 'well he wakes up first of all and um + he's angry with the monkeys' (lines 7–8). Now the learner seems to have identified the correct picture, 'ah yeah' (line 9). But the teacher double-checks that he has understood with 'because + yes?' (line 10). Even though the learner seems to confirm that with 'ah yes' (line 11), the teacher explicitly fills in the causal link ('because they've taken his hats' at line 12) and finally

repeats the original problematic phrase with a further explicit reformulation ('and he + shakes his fist that is he waves his arm + at them',
line 14).

This extract is a good example of how much the partners in a conversation may rely on each other for positive and negative clues as to 'where
they have got to' on the way to understanding.

# Modifications of information choice

Most research into the way native speakers modify what they say for non-
native listeners has concentrated on modifications of input and/or interaction. But there is also some evidence of a third type of modification:
information choice. Two North American studies of native–non-native
conversation have revealed some of the forms it can take. First, when asked
to talk to a non-native partner, native speakers tend to select more concrete and more immediate topics in free conversation (Long 1983).
Second, in a study where the conversational topic was fixed in advance,
it was found that native speakers modified by giving weaker non-native
listeners more background detail (Derwing 1989).

Those two studies involved native speakers in general. The modifications
of information made by language teachers in particular have been
analysed in the story-telling experiment mentioned earlier in this chapter
(Lynch 1986). It found that native EFL teachers, as well as modifying
input and interaction, adjusted both the amount and the type of information they gave to intermediate and elementary-level learners, in three
ways:

- increasing the quantity of descriptive detail
- making the logical links in the story explicit
- filling in assumed gaps in socio-cultural knowledge.

I will briefly give you some examples of these aspects of teachers' selection of information.

## *Descriptive detail*

The teachers in the experiment described characters and actions in more
detail to help their lower-proficiency listeners follow the story. In one of
the stories, a blind beggar appears in the second of the six pictures, shown
below:

*Figure 3.2* (from Heaton 1966)

Example 3.7 shows how a male Scottish teacher described the beggar's arrival on the scene to his four listeners. (I have underlined the individual bits of information.)

**Example 3.7**

| | |
|---|---|
| *Native:* | 'and he notices this <u>blind</u> <u>beggar</u>' (2 bits) |
| *Advanced:* | 'and he can see a <u>blind</u> <u>beggar</u> + with a <u>hat</u> + and a <u>sign</u> around his + coat saying <u>BLIND</u>' (5 bits of information) |
| *Intermediate:* | 'and he sees + a <u>blind</u> <u>beggar</u> + with a <u>hat</u> + and a <u>cup</u> + and a <u>stick</u> + and <u>dark</u> <u>glasses</u> + and a <u>sign</u> around his neck which says <u>BLIND</u>' (8 bits) |
| *Elementary:* | 'he sees + an <u>old</u> + <u>blind</u> + <u>beggar</u> *(long pause)* <u>blind</u> <u>beggar</u> with a <u>hat</u> + and a <u>cup</u> + and a <u>sign</u> that says <u>BLIND</u> + and a <u>stick</u> in his <u>hand</u> + and he sees this <u>old</u> <u>blind</u> <u>beggar</u>' |

(14 bits of information, including repetitions)

That overall pattern is typical of the way many teachers introduced characters in the stories. They mentioned more details, and repeated them more often, to the elementary-level listeners than to their other three partners. They offered fewest details and least repetition to their fellow native speakers. One natural result of modifying for the weaker listeners by providing more detail is that some bits of information were mentioned only to the elementary learners. In Example 3.7, it was the fact that the blind man was <u>old</u>. All but one of the 24 teachers who took part in the experiment modified their choice of information in this way.

Offering such detailed additional information to low-proficiency listeners carries a risk: it may not fulfil its aim of making communication easier. In Chapter 1 I referred to Craig Chaudron's research into teachers' explanation of vocabulary, which highlighted the danger of 'swamping' the listener with information. I will come back to this potential problem in the next chapter.

## Logical links

The second form of modification of information choice concerns the degree to which the teachers made explicit the logical links in the story. In Example 3.8 you can compare the versions told by a female English teacher to explain why the blind man was begging.

*Example 3.8*

| | |
|---|---|
| *Native:* | 'the blind man . . . he's obviously rattling his tin to try and beg from passers-by' |
| *Advanced:* | 'it's a blind man + shaking a + tin + to try and beg for money from passers-by' |
| *Intermediate:* | 'an old man + shaking a tin + this tin is to collect money + from the people in the street + <u>because this man is blind</u> + <u>he can't see anything</u> + and <u>he hasn't got a job</u> + he <u>needs somebody to give him money</u> + <u>so that he can live</u>' |
| *Elementary:* | 'the blind man has a tin and he's rattling the tin <u>in order to attract people's attention</u> because <u>he wants them to give him some money</u> + <u>because he's blind and he's poor he can't work</u>' |

The underlined sections show how this teacher gave more and more explanation as the level of her listener went down. For the intermediate and elementary listeners, she spelt out the cause-and-effect chain underlying the man's actions (being blind → having no job → being poor → having to beg). She did not mention any of those links to her native and advanced listeners. Apparently she expected lower-level learners to be less able to work out these (relatively simple) connections for themselves.

You may also have noticed that she used the word 'obviously' only to her native partner, which I find interesting. A number of teachers in this study used this and similar expressions (e.g. 'of course', 'naturally', 'surprise, surprise') exclusively in the native versions of their stories, which suggest that they thought native listeners would have ready access to the knowledge required to make sense of the story and even to predict events, actions, and characters' feelings.

This can be accounted for by the 'speech accommodation theory' that I mentioned in Chapter 1. By using phrases like 'obviously', the teachers were indicating that they felt their relationship with their fellow native speakers was different from that with the learners of English—even though the setting and task were identical in all four cases. In other words, they 'converged' towards their native partners; they felt able to leave things unsaid, in the confident belief that the message would still get through. By contrast, in the native–non-native conversations, they 'diverged' from their listeners by spelling out the logical links.

Although the teacher in Example 3.8 may have had the best of intentions in making the modifications she did, there is a risk that our efforts to make something clear will sound patronizing or even insulting to the learners. I will be discussing this point in more detail in Chapter 4.

## *Assumed socio-cultural gaps*

Almost half the teachers in the experiment provided extra socio-cultural information for the weaker listeners. Take the case of two gestures made by the hat seller in pictures 4 and 5 of the monkey story (see page 40): fist-shaking and head-scratching. As far as I have been able to find out (by asking people from a variety of cultures), head-scratching is a universal gesture. Nevertheless, in the case of picture 5, ten teachers thought they needed to help the linguistically weaker partners with a socio-cultural explanation of why people scratch their heads, as in the case of another male Scottish teacher (Example 3.9).

*Example 3.9*
>  *Native:* 'this was rather puzzling + so he takes off his hat and scratches his head'
>
>  *Advanced:* 'and he takes off his hat and scratches his head + in confusion'
>
>  *Intermediate:* 'well the man doesn't know what to do + he's very puzzled + and so he scratches his head <u>which means I don't know what to do</u>'
>
>  *Elementary:* 'the old man is + very puzzled and worried about + how to get his hats + from the monkeys *(pause)* and he takes off his hat and scratches his head + <u>as people often do + when they feel puzzled</u>'

A number of the teachers provided similar explanations for the fist-shaking gesture in picture 4 of the same story. Again, it was only the weaker listeners, and especially those at elementary level, who were given this explicit guidance on how to interpret the man's action. The teachers seemed to assume that someone with a good command of a language is bound to have knowledge of the relevant socio-cultural information.

To sum up, teachers in the story-telling experiment modified more for intermediate and elementary learners than for advanced and native listeners. For listeners at the two lowest levels, they described characters and objects in more detail, made the causal links more explicit, and provided help with socio-cultural interpretations more often than to the advanced and native listeners. When you recall that the listeners in the experiment had all the pictures in front of them (and so were not completely dependent on the teacher's words), then the degree of modification these teachers adopted was even more striking.

# Implications for classroom practice

We have seen that teachers try to make things easier for learners either by preventing comprehension problems or by remedying them as they occur. Prevention involves modifying unfamiliar input; remedy is possible through interaction, provided the learners indicate they are in difficulty. In either case, the clear message from research is that it takes longer to put a message across to elementary learners than to the more advanced. Although intuition might tell us that a shorter message is easier to understand than a longer one, the evidence is that—assuming the content remains the same—teachers need to use more words (and therefore take more time) when talking to elementary learners. Rather than being tempted to think that some students are 'slow to understand', it is more sensible to recognize that we have to allow ourselves the time to make successful modifications.

A second implication is that, for interaction modifications to work, there has to be *genuine* interaction between teachers and learners. Interacting is more than taking turns to speak. It requires attention to what the other people are saying. You may have observed some teachers who pepper their classroom talk with 'OK' and 'all right'; on the face of it, they seem to be checking learners' comprehension. But then they do not leave enough time for the learners to respond before they go on to their next point. They are paying lip service to interaction.

The third implication arising from research is that interactive negotiation of meaning with a group of students is bound to be less straightforward than when talking to just one listener. Rod Ellis has made the point that the teacher has to base decisions about modification on a subjective assessment of the class's overall level of proficiency. As a result, Teacher Talk is likely to be less finely tuned to the level of the learners than is possible in one-to-one conversation (Ellis 1985).

Nevertheless, if we create a classroom atmosphere in which students feel free to make clear when they find it hard to follow what is said, we have a better basis for deciding when and how we should modify. We saw in the set of extracts from the parallel listening lessons (Examples 3.3 to 3.5) that two of the teachers were able to make successful modifications by encouraging learners' participation in the process of communication. In Example 3.5 the teacher with the post-elementary class repeated and reformulated her instructions, and then checked that her students had understood. But we cannot be sure, simply by reading the transcript, precisely *what* made her aware that modification was called for. Perhaps she noticed that not all the students joined in the chorus of 'yeah' when she asked 'ok?' Perhaps she saw one or two students frowning or turning to their neighbours for help. Whatever the clues were that this teacher picked up in the students' reactions, the important thing is that she responded by making the necessary modifications. Negotiation of meaning in the classroom requires confidence on the learners' part and sensitivity on the teacher's.

Overall, as I will show in Chapter 4, research suggests that interaction modifications are *potentially* more helpful than input modifications alone, but we need to use them carefully if they are *actually* to help learners understand. Modifications should not become part of an automatic classroom routine; they need to be consciously integrated into the way we communicate with learners.

# Summary

In this chapter I have described three types of modification used in Teacher Talk, intended to assist learners' comprehension. Teachers employ a combination of adjustments to language form (input) and to conversational structure (interaction), and there is also some evidence that we choose different types and amounts of information when talking to intermediate- and elementary-level learners than to more advanced students.

Researchers have gradually built up a picture of the modifications teachers make. But do they actually work? As Craig Chaudron put it, the final test of Teacher Talk is the practical one of whether the modifications result in information being effectively understood and remembered (Chaudron 1983).

Are some types of modification more effective than others? For instance, does repetition lead to better comprehension than reformulation? Could it be that some types of modification in fact hamper comprehension rather than improve it? Is there any evidence that specific forms of modification lead to better longer-term progress? In Chapter 4 I review research into the relative benefits of the listener-orientated modifications discussed in this chapter.

## *Suggestions for further reading*

### *Participation in the language classroom*

**Johnson, K.** 1995. *Understanding Communication in the Second Language Classroom.* Cambridge: Cambridge University Press. This book draws on social and educational research to give a comprehensive account of the factors shaping learners' and teachers' perceptions of classroom events.

**Malamah-Thomas, A.** 1987. *Classroom Interaction.* Oxford: Oxford University Press. A less theoretical book than Johnson's, exploring the relationship between teaching purpose and classroom language. It includes suggestions and materials for observing teachers at work.

### *Teacher Talk*

Several books include chapters on Teacher Talk in wider surveys of language learning research. The most recent is **Ellis, R.** 1994. *The Study of Second Language Acquisition.* Oxford: Oxford University Press (Chapter 7).

# 4 MODIFICATION RESEARCH: FINDINGS AND IMPLICATIONS

This chapter presents the results of research into what happens when teachers modify what they say to learners and whether it actually aids comprehension. Much of the research into how native speakers modify their speech to non-native speakers has been based on the assumption that once the message is modified so as to make it comprehensible, the learner may then pick up and later use new items of language contained in the message. Perhaps the clearest expression of this assumption is that of Michael Long, who argued that research into the connection between input, interaction, and learning would have to be based on a three-step argument:

1 Show that discourse modifications promote the comprehension of input
2 Show that comprehensible input promotes learning
3 Deduce that discourse modifications promote learning.
(Long 1985: 378)

Since a major reason for investigating modifications (Step 1) was a concern with the processes that lead to comprehension, one might have expected that researchers would have wanted from the beginning to measure the effects of modification on learners' understanding. Yet it is only in the last ten years or so that researchers have measured the comprehension effects of various types of modification and have investigated whether some modifications help more than others.

## Problems of measurement

Assessing the success of discourse modifications is not a straightforward matter, whether in the classroom or elsewhere. It may have been partly for this reason that research into native–non-native communication was initially limited to descriptions of the native speakers' performance. This quotation from one early study shows that the assessment of any benefits for the non-native listener was a matter of guesswork:

> The modifications made by [the native speakers] in our sample *do appear to simplify and facilitate communication.* Our evidence . . . is *indirect.* We *cannot be sure* that the particular syntactic structures and lexical items that they avoided were those that *would have given* non-native listeners the most difficulty. However, it is *reasonable to suppose* that shorter, grammatically simpler sentences using a more limited vocabulary and expressing simpler ideas are easier to understand.
> (Arthur *et al.* 1980: 123, my emphasis)

Such evaluation of learners' comprehension of modified discourse was subjective and impressionistic. Even the 'reasonable supposition' that grammatically simpler sentences are easier to understand is dubious. For example, as I mentioned in Chapter 2, research into simplification has found that learners understand some reading texts containing short, grammatically simple sentences less well than they understand more complex texts containing relative and time clauses (Johnson 1982). So we cannot assume that *restrictive* or *linguistic simplification* will lead to greater comprehensibility.

Although what is true for reading is not necessarily true for listening, Patricia Johnson's study underlines the general point that comprehension should be *measured* and not taken for granted. Barbara Hawkins made a similar comment about the risk of drawing firm conclusions on the basis of impressions: 'We cannot make strong claims about *how* Foreigner Talk aids learners in their comprehension if we do not know *what* they comprehend' (Hawkins 1985: 176). Her point is well illustrated, I think, in the classroom episode in the Activity below.

## *Activity*

### What do students understand?

In Example 4.1 an Irish teacher is working with a group of elementary-level learners of English, all of whom have Arabic as their first language. As we join them, the teacher is going through a word list in their coursebook before moving on to a dialogue task in which they will be using the words listed.

What evidence can you find in the transcript that the teacher's attempt to explain the word 'excursion' is successful, i.e. that she has made the word comprehensible to the learners? (I have underlined the teacher's attempts at explanation.)

*Example 4.1*

T   So em we have new words: train, buses, plane, boat and excursion. What is an excursion, Maudhir? What is an <u>excursion</u>?

N   *(mutters)* an excursion

T   Do you know?

M   Where is it?

T   An excursion. It's one of the words here.

M   Excur- excursion. Same. Like ship.

T   No, it's not. It's, do you know what's to go on <u>a tour</u>? For example, you sometimes spend a day going round Edinburgh, ok? You go round and have a look at all the famous sites. That's to go around—take a tour round Edinburgh. And go on an excursion means <u>you go away, usually for a day</u>, for, you go, you, you go from, say, you might go from here to Glasgow for an excursion. That means you might leave here in the morning, go over to Glasgow, go and see all the famous places in Glasgow and come back. That is an excursion.

N   *(to the other students)* temshi *(waggling his hand)*

T   So it is <u>a journey</u>. You go away . . .

M   Why?

T   . . . somewhere. You go, you go, yes em, an excursion usually means . . .

M   Visit?

T   . . . eh, you go to a place <u>to visit</u>, yeah, the area to look around the town, to go on an excursion.

Ss  *(talk to each other in Arabic)*

T   For example, just before Christmas, all the students here went on an excursion to Glasgow. They went over to the museum and they visited the museum in Glasgow, and then they came back. And that's an excursion. Where you <u>go away for a while</u>.

M   See expidation.

T   To see an exhibition, yes, to see an exhibition. So to go on an excursion is what you say. So if you were to go on an excursion to Glasgow, you would have to . . .
    *(moves to next teaching point)*

(adapted from Parkinson 1986)

It is easy enough to follow the teacher's attempts to make clear the meaning of 'excursion'. She uses a variety of modifications: she repeats the word and reformulates it, puts it into context, and links it with the learners' own experience. In fact she does her best to exploit the learners' knowledge at any of the three information levels shown in Figure 2.1 on page 20 (language, context, and background).

But it is much more difficult to be sure of how much—and even whether—the students understand. There are some signs that the teacher's modifications are having the intended effect. For example, student N offers his fellow learners an Arabic translation, *temshi*, but the way he waggles his hand at the same time suggests that he is himself not sure. In fact, it was only in the course of writing this book that I learnt from my colleague Eileen Dwyer that *temshi* is the Arabic for 'you go'. So what learner N seems to have picked up from the teacher's modifications is her repeated use of the words 'you' and 'go', which she mentions ten times, either separately or together. N has noticed what the teacher has said most often.

We do not know whether the teacher hears what N says and, if she does, whether she realizes he is speaking Arabic. After she has mentioned the recent school trip to Glasgow as an example, another student suggests 'see expidation', which she interprets as 'to see an exhibition'. It could be, however, that the student is suggesting the word 'expedition' as a paraphrase for 'excursion'.

That extract shows how difficult it can be to assess what sense learners are making of input in a language lesson—in this case, a combination of written text (the item on the printed word list) and speech (the questions and explanations from the teacher).

## Effects on comprehension

Given the difficulty of judging precisely what listeners understand of a modified message, a large number of research studies have been designed to pin down the effects of modifications—which modifications help comprehension, to what extent, at which levels of proficiency, and so on. I will briefly review some of the main findings of research featuring learners of English.

# Input modifications

Among the topics investigated in studies that have isolated and measured the effects on listeners' comprehension of *specific* features of native–non-native input modification are:

- ways of highlighting the topic
- repetition
- rate of speaking
- syntactic simplification
- elaboration.

## Study 1: Highlighting the topic

Craig Chaudron studied the effects of different versions of a short lecture on the comprehension of 135 learners at low, intermediate, and advanced levels on an intensive English programme at Boston University (Chaudron 1983). The lectures were scripted to include references to sub-topics of the main theme, which were mentioned and then later referred to again ('reinstated') twice.

Chaudron measured comprehension by the learners' performance on two types of comprehension question (recall and recognition). Of five types of reinstatement tested, it was repetition of the noun that had the strongest measurable effect on comprehension. But Chaudron also found that although repeating the noun was the most effective modification for the two lower-proficiency groups, for the more advanced listeners it had no greater effect than the four other types of reinstatement. So it may be that different sorts of modification assist different levels of learners: more proficient listeners do not require as much redundancy—additional information in the form or repetition or reformulation—as learners at lower levels.

## Study 2: Repetition

The suggestion that redundancy of information makes understanding easier for learners at relatively low levels of proficiency is supported by the results of a dictation experiment. One of Chaudron's graduate students in Hawaii, Raoul Cervantes, carried out an experiment with 16 intermediate-level learners of English (Cervantes 1983). Half the group heard a dictation text once only; the other half heard it twice. This simple repetition—in this case, of every part of the text—enabled the learners who heard the text twice to achieve significantly higher dictation scores.

This may seem unsurprising to language teachers, but it is worth reflecting on precisely *how* repetition of the text helps a learner to get a better dictation score. One possibility is that when learners know they will have the opportunity to hear something twice, the first hearing acts as an 'advance organizer' for the second. It helps them to identify the parts of the text they cannot easily understand, so that they can pay particular attention to them the second time around. Another advantage of repetition is that if the students know they will be able to hear the message twice, they may feel more relaxed. We know from learner diary studies that anxiety can be a particular obstacle in listening comprehension. Simply relaxing may well increase performance in understanding.

### Studies 3 and 4: Rate of speaking

Another common-sense notion about native–non-native modification is that it helps listeners if we slow down. But how much does it help? Does slow speech help by itself, or only when it is combined with other modifications? In another Hawaiian study, Ken Kelch compared intermediate students' success in understanding one of four versions of a dictation text: (A) unmodified; (B) spoken slowly; (C) grammatically simplified in ways typical of Foreigner Talk; and (D) version C spoken slowly (Kelch 1985). The subjects of the study were 26 students taking degree programmes and also attending part-time courses in English at the University of Hawaii. Their dictation scripts were marked in two ways, one method focusing on form and the other on meaning. On both measures, reduced speaking rate was shown to assist comprehension. However, version D, which combined both types of modification, increased listeners' scores only when assessed for meaning, not for form. Kelch concluded that this difference might be linked to the distinction between messages that are cognitively simpler rather than linguistically simpler (see Chapter 1). Possibly the grammatical adjustments in versions C and D made them cognitively simpler and more accessible in terms of meaning. So they helped listeners to understand them better, but made exact recall of form less easy.

Using a different measure of listening comprehension (true/false questions rather than dictation) and working with EFL learners in Oman, Roger Griffiths carried out a series of experiments on the effect of rate of speaking. One involved playing recordings of short stories to 24 Omani teachers of English, whose average listening proficiency was lower-intermediate (Griffiths 1990). The stories had been recorded at different rates of speaking: moderately fast (around 200 words a minute), average (150 words a minute) and slow (100 words a minute). Griffiths found that at this level of proficiency in English, the learners understood information spoken at the average rate significantly better than when it was presented at the higher rate. However, their comprehension was no better at 100 words a minute than at 150 words a minute. Griffiths drew two conclusions: (1) there seemed to be an optimum rate of speaking, above which learners at this level would begin to miss or mishear some information; (2) really slow speech brings no gain in comprehension.

## Study 5: Syntactic simplification

Surprisingly, until quite recently nobody had studied the specific effects of grammatical simplification on listening comprehension. Raoul Cervantes and Glenn Gainer carried out two experiments at Fukuoka University in Japan, to compare the comprehensibility resulting from syntactic simplification and from repetition (Cervantes and Gainer 1992). One experiment involved 76 students majoring in English, at varying levels of proficiency, who heard two versions of a lecture which differed in the number of subordinate clauses they contained. Results of a cloze test (a gap-filling test) showed that those who had heard the syntactically simpler version scored higher.

In the second experiment, learners' comprehension was tested by dictation. It was carried out with a separate group of 82 students, majoring in English like those in the first study, who heard one of three versions of another lecture: version 1 had few subordinate clauses; version 2 had more; version 3 was the same as the second, but with repetition. The students' scores indicated that version 1 (syntactically modified) and version 3 (repeated) were both easier than version 2 (no simplification or repetition). There was no measurable difference between the students' comprehension of versions 1 and 3. So both forms of modification helped, and to the same degree.

## Study 6: Elaboration

Most input research has been carried out with students who are either studying English in a second-language context such as the United States, or are majoring in English at a university. One of the few input modification studies involving non-specialist learners in an EFL context was conducted at the Naval Academy in Taiwan. Chung Shing Chiang and Patricia Dunkel investigated the relative effects on comprehension of three factors: input modifications, subject knowledge, and listening proficiency level (Chiang and Dunkel 1992). The participants in the experiment were a group of 360 undergraduates at intermediate level, who listened to unmodified or elaborated versions of two short lectures and then answered a variety of comprehension questions. Some could be answered by direct reference to the lecturer's words and others would require the listeners to interpret meaning.

After taking into account the students' subject knowledge and listening proficiency, Chiang and Dunkel were able to show that elaboration helped the higher-level students but not the weaker ones. So this provided further support for Chaudron's argument that discourse modifications help comprehension to different degrees according to the learner's overall level in the language.

## Relevance to the classroom

As always, we have to be cautious about looking for what research might
'tell us' about the classroom. In many cases the ingredients of research
experiments (the type of learners, the texts used, the comprehension measures, etc.) are so specific to the context that it would not be reasonable
to base classroom practice on the findings. The research studies of input
modifications mentioned in this section share three limitations, from the
point of view of the teacher looking for immediate guidance on how to
talk to learners. Firstly, they involved listening to *scripted* texts, rather than
the *spontaneous* speech typical of classroom talk. By controlling the content and form of the different lecture versions, the researchers were able
to isolate and compare the effects of alternative forms of input modification, but with the result that the language they investigated was unlike
what a speaker would produce naturally.

A second point to bear in mind is that the ways in which listeners' comprehension is measured in these input modification studies imply a single
type of listening, in which the aim is to achieve *total* comprehension. This
is especially true of research in which assessment of comprehension is
based on dictation tests, where success is judged in terms of word-for-
word reproduction of the original message. It is true that we do occasionally need to take dictation in real life, but to use it as the only
measurement of comprehension is to exaggerate the importance of preci-
sion in listening. In real life, we rarely need to understand 100 per cent
of a spoken message. It is even questionable whether that level of comprehension is possible—as I suggested in my discussion of pragmatic
meaning in Chapter 2.

The third limitation is that most research has concentrated on one type
of listening text: lecture-style talks. Again, this has to do with the
researchers' wish to focus on input. Lectures predominantly involve one-
way communication from speaker to listener, with students exerting
little control over what the lecturer says, so they provide perhaps the most
natural setting for study of the effects of input modification. At first sight,
lectures are not the obvious place to look for insights into teacher–learner
communication in the language classroom, but in fact a language lesson
and a lecture actually have a great deal in common. Firstly, the purpose
of both is educational, so that the relationships between lecturer and students, and teacher and learners, are similar—much more so, for instance,
than the relationship between native and non-native speakers talking outside the classroom. Secondly, in both settings the lecturer/teacher is the
main speaker, although recent changes in approach have made some language classrooms more interactive. In fact, we should remember that in
many places, for reasons to do with material resources or educational cul-

ture, the language lesson may well resemble a lecture. So we should not assume that we can easily separate 'lecture' from 'lesson'. It is not a case of black and white differences, rather shades of grey. So there are arguments for saying that what the two settings share is much greater than what divides them.

## Implications for classroom practice

Input modification experiments offer possible insights into ways in which we should talk to learners. At the very least, the research has shown the advantages and disadvantages of certain modifications; it is useful for teachers to know, for example, that speaking very slowly does not always make listening easier, and that repetition may be as helpful as grammatical simplification. The main difference between lessons and lectures is that learners in the language class probably have the opportunity to get meanings clarified as comprehension problems arise. So we need to look to studies of interaction modifications for insight into the possible benefits of adjusting the structure of teacher–learner talk to increase comprehension.

# *Interaction modifications*

### *Study 7: Interaction versus input*

The first published study to compare the benefits of teachers' adjustment of input and interaction in classroom discourse was the one by Teresa Pica, Richard Young, and Catherine Doughty that I mentioned in Chapter 3 (Pica, Young, and Doughty 1987). They wanted to test the claim that learners achieve better understanding through interaction than by hearing a message 'pre-packaged' in linguistically simplified form.

The participants in their research were 16 low-intermediate learners on a general English programme at the University of Pennsylvania. They were divided into two groups and carried out an information-gap task in which they had to arrange various objects on a board in response to spoken instructions from a female native speaker (not a teacher). Listeners and speaker sat face to face, with screens preventing them from seeing each other's boards. Each group heard either an 'input' version or an 'interaction' version of the instructions.

In the input version, the instructor read out a text and paused to allow the listeners time to carry out each instruction. The script for the teacher's text was based on recordings of native speakers doing the task, but with some linguistic modifications added. In the interaction version, she read an unmodified script but encouraged the listeners to ask her for repetition, clarification, and so on when necessary.

The results supported the authors' hypothesis that interaction assists learners more than modified input. The listeners who had the opportunity to interact with the teacher scored higher (by selecting and placing the objects more accurately) than those who received the *pre-modified* instructions. Interaction modifications were also the most effective way of dealing with serious comprehension problems, and there was evidence that, of the various types of interaction modification, it was repetition that helped listeners most.

### Study 8: Observing interaction

In a classroom study related to the story-telling research described in Chapter 3, I investigated whether learners who observe a recording of native–non-native conversation also gain similar benefits to those of the original non-native partner, in terms of better comprehension of the story (Lynch 1988a). The reason for looking at this issue was an interest in designing comprehension materials: if classroom learners can take advantage at second hand, so to speak, of interaction modifications, it would be possible to use recordings of successful native–non-native conversations as comprehension material.

You may recall that in the first stage of this research I had video-taped 24 native teachers telling picture-based stories to four levels of listener: native, advanced, intermediate, and elementary. The second stage took the form of a comprehension experiment involving 222 elementary-level Portuguese learners of English, who were attending part-time English courses at the British Institute in Lisbon. The experimental materials were videotapes of sixteen versions of one story told by four teachers to their four partners. I selected the recordings by these teachers on two grounds: their success in helping all four original listeners to number the six pictures correctly; and their individual style of modification to their intermediate- and elementary-level partners. Without prompting or practice, two of the four teachers had adopted an 'input' style for the weaker listeners, using more common vocabulary, simplified grammar, and pausing more often; the other two teachers had used an 'interactive' style of storytelling, in which they regularly checked listeners' comprehension and responded to their queries.

The Portuguese learners' comprehension of the videotaped stories was tested as part of a normal English class. Each learner was given a set of five of the six pictures on which the story was based, in jumbled order and with the final picture missing. Their task was in two parts: (1) to number the pictures to match the story they watched and heard; and (2) to write in Portuguese what happened at the end of the story (i.e. in the sixth picture). The results showed that their understanding of the events in the story was assisted most by watching the version told to the listeners at or near their own level in English. The benefit was greater for those who watched a story told in the more interactive style, rather than one in which the teacher had tended towards a 'monologue' of simplified input. So this study found evidence that elementary learners listening under 'real' class-room conditions (in regular classes and to unscripted comprehension materials) also benefited from the sort of interactive modifications that other researchers had studied under more controlled conditions.

### Study 9: Participating versus observing

In an extension of the Pennsylvania experiment, using the same experi-mental method, Teresa Pica compared the performances of 24 learners working on the layout task in one of three classroom roles (Pica 1991). Eight Negotiators heard the unmodified instructions and were encouraged to request help from the speaker when necessary. Eight Observers per-formed the task at the same time as the Negotiators, heard the same instructions, and were able to witness the negotiation, but could not par-ticipate in it themselves. Eight Listeners completed the task separately from the Negotiators and Observers; the instructions they heard were different from those to the other two groups, being read aloud from the script incorporating typical input modifications. They were not allowed to ask for help or repetition.

Pica had expected to find that first-hand negotiation would lead to bet-ter comprehension than second-hand observation of interaction, which in turn would bring greater success than listening to modified input. What she in fact found was that the Negotiators did slightly better than both Observers and Listeners, but there was no difference between the scores of Observers and Listeners. Pica's study offers another piece of evidence that active face-to-face negotiation between learners and teacher offers a more efficient route to listening comprehension than listening to pre-packaged modified input.

## Relevance to the classroom

These three research studies suggest that allowing opportunities for inter-action, which leads on to the negotiation of meaning, offers a more effect-ive way of assisting learners' comprehension. Apart from improved understanding, they will gain experience in taking the initiative in getting communication problems sorted out.

However, there are two obvious ways in which the picture of teacher–learner interaction shown in the studies of interaction modification is untypical of most classrooms: class size and classroom culture.

Even the 'classroom' studies summarized in this section involved com-paratively small groups of learners (eight in the Pennsylvania experiments and up to 16 in a class in Lisbon). So how relevant are the findings to a teacher facing a class of 40 or more in a secondary school? Again, it is important here not to see things in black or white terms. Allowing more interaction with learners, and encouraging them to ask for clarification and other forms of help when meaning is unclear, does not necessarily mean a chaotic free-for-all. For example, Karuna Kumar of the Central Institute for English and Foreign Languages in Hyderabad studied how English teachers interacted with large and small classes (45 and 25 learners, respectively) at an Indian middle school (Kumar 1992). He found that class size was less important than the way the teacher encouraged or limited interaction. The teacher working with a large class was actually able to generate more talk from her pupils than one with small numbers. Yet, as Kumar's transcripts show, their contributions were orderly and relevant to the task.

By careful planning and appropriate selection of the classroom activity (play reading and role play) the teacher was able to create interaction in which pupils participated, not just by requesting help when they needed it but also commenting, joking, and making suggestions. But as Kumar argues, it is not a case of having to decide for *either* interaction-based *or* traditional teacher-fronted activity; both are necessary parts of the teaching programme.

The other objection to interaction-based teaching is one that questions the cultural assumptions in patterns of classroom participation. Almost all research into the effects of interaction modifications is North American; it features adult learners attending full-time courses in English as a second language; and it is conducted in a university environment. So it naturally reflects the values of American educational culture (e.g. individual rights and personal growth), which may be inappropriate for younger learners, those on non-academic courses, or in other cultures. If we take the role of the teacher as an example, it is clear that the 'humanistic' movement towards regarding the teacher as consultant, informant, guide, and facilitator—rather than as the authoritative source of knowledge and wisdom—may not be at all relevant in cultures with a different educational philosophy. So above all, we have to adapt in a way that suits the local environment. This is one reason why Karuna Kumar's classroom study is of particular interest, since it shows teachers using interaction-based classroom techniques outside what I will call the Anglo-Saxon context, in a way that is recognizably local.

## Implications for classroom practice

One area in which interaction modification research might have something to say to teachers is in the design of materials and tasks for listening comprehension. The results from my study suggest that learners watching recordings of interaction between native and non-native speakers gained from the original listener's negotiation of meaning. In many cases—perhaps the majority of the world's classrooms—teachers do not have easy access to English language broadcasts or to commercial listening materials. The interaction research suggests that teachers could produce their own comprehension material, assuming that they have access to three basic 'resources': a cassette recorder (video, if possible); a native or competent speaker of the target language; and a learner at roughly the same level as the learners with whom the recording will be used. Assuming these elements are available, it would not simply be a matter of turning on the recorder and telling the two people to talk. To ensure that the conversation contains the sort of modifications that are required, the two people would have to be asked to carry out a practical task (such as placing objects or marking a grid). The listener should be encouraged to give feedback (negative and positive) so that the speaker knows when to make modifications for comprehension. In this way it is possible for the teacher to set up the right conditions in which the speaker will tailor the input to the listener.

## Modifications of information choice

Among the findings of the story-telling study mentioned in Chapter 3 (Lynch 1986) was that native teachers of English spontaneously adjusted their selection of information to help intermediate- and elementary-level learners. They did this in three ways: giving fuller descriptions of people, making links between events explicit, and filling in assumed gaps in socio-cultural knowledge. In this section I will summarize research into two potential effects of speakers' information choice: on learners' *comprehension* and on their *self-perception*. On both counts, it seems that when native speakers modify the content of what they say, there can be negative repercussions.

### Learners' comprehension

#### Study 10: Effects on comprehension
Tracy Derwing of the University of Alberta conducted a story-telling experiment with 16 pairs of native and non-native speakers of English (Derwing 1989). The native speakers were shown a silent animated film, chosen because of the unexpected twists and turns of its story. Each native speaker was then asked to retell the story from memory to another native speaker and to a low-intermediate learner. The listeners' understanding of the story was tested with six comprehension questions. Derwing analysed the information mentioned in the narratives into three categories: *crucial*

(information needed to answer the test questions), *major* (information that provided coherence to the story), and *minor* (background detail not directly related to a specific event in the story). The listeners' test scores showed that crucial information had a significant effect on listeners' comprehension, as one might expect. The second finding was that unsuccessful narrators (those whose listeners scored 50 per cent or less on the test) had used significantly less major information. Thirdly, minor background details had a negative effect on comprehension.

Derwing's research suggests that learners stand a better chance of understanding a story if they are told the key events in an explicitly coherent way. However, their level of understanding may fall if the narrator gives them too much background detail—even if this is done with the best of intentions.

## Learners' self-perceptions

In her conclusion, Derwing quotes a comment from an earlier study of modification: 'Too much information is more confusing than too little, or at least it gives people a stronger *feeling* of being confused' (Dahl 1981: 87, emphasis added). The way that learners feel about communication with native speakers is something I am particularly interested in. One reason is that, as a native speaker married to a non-native speaker of English, I am regularly made aware of the way British people can mistakenly assume that non-native speakers do not have certain sorts of background knowledge. Secondly, most of the students I teach are either about to start, or have started, university courses in Scotland. They often tell me of their feelings of frustration when native speakers talk to them in a way which implies that their problem is a lack of knowledge or intelligence, and not simply an imperfect command of English.

Peter Harder of the University of Copenhagen has described how you feel when you are trying to express yourself in a language you do not know well. The title of his paper, 'On the reduced personality of the second language learner' (Harder 1981), summarizes his view very clearly. He says that frustration is unfortunate but inevitable: 'in order to be a wit in a foreign language you have to go through the stage of being a half-wit' (Harder 1981: 269). Looking at the learner's self-image from the perspective of listening, a number of writers have speculated that when native speakers modify in an exaggerated way, the result may be that the non-native listener feels patronized. For example, have a look at the reaction of this elementary learner to the 'help' he is offered by the native speaker of English, in the form of additional information.

*Example 4.2*
   S  and on the other side of the road + from the shop + there
      was a blind man + a man with + dark glasses + holding
   L  a man who + sorry?
   S  yes?
   L  a man                                               5
   S  a blind man
   L  <u>a blind man yes I see</u>
   S  a blind man yes he has a stick in his hand + and uh + dark
      glasses
   L  <u>hmhm OK</u>                                      10
   S  and he was holding + a + a can can in his hand + to collect
      money
   L  <u>yeah yeah + I see</u>
   S  yeah? + + so the little boy noticed him . . .
(experimental data)

Despite the listener's signals that he has understood, the speaker continues to add further description and explanation. 'Yeah yeah + I see' (line 13) is the learner's third attempt to show he has got the point, and even then the speaker checks again before continuing. Either she does not recognize her partner's signals, or she is ignoring them.

*Study 11: Effects on learners' perceptions*
In an exploratory study, I looked into this issue of 'speaking up or talking down'. I asked a group of learners to eavesdrop on a native–non-native-speaker conversation, to see whether the native speaker's exaggerated modifications of information affected their attitudes to speaker and listener (Lynch 1988b). The subjects in the study were 19 students, from intermediate to advanced, taking an academic English course at the University of Edinburgh. They were played two audio-recordings of a story told by the same English teacher to a native listener and an elementary-level learner. I then asked them for their impressions of various characteristics of the speaker and listener in the two recordings (e.g. age, friendliness, intelligence). I did not reveal the circumstances in which the stories were taped, or the origins of the partners.

The learners' comments showed that the majority of the listeners thought that the elementary listener was a child, while most thought the native listener was an adult. Interestingly, the speaker's tone of voice and presentation were so different in the two versions that almost a third of the listeners did not realize that it was the same person. Among their comments was one that the recording sounded like a psychiatric interview.

This was an informal experiment with a small group of mixed levels, and I make no claim that the teacher's behaviour was typical—either of teachers in general, or even of this particular teacher. In fact, my reason for choosing recordings by that particular teacher was that she had adopted what I called an 'overkill' strategy, giving much more detail than seemed necessary. But the experiment provides a useful reminder for teachers that some of our modifications for learners, especially adjustments of content, risk being perceived as patronizing and not simply well-meaning.

## Implications for classroom practice

The Alberta and Edinburgh studies reported in this section underline the fact that the relationship between content modification and comprehension is not straightforward. We cannot take it for granted that the more information we give, the better our students will understand us. When we are trying to explain something, it is perhaps natural to provide more detail, in the expectation that a more complete picture will help. But Tracy Derwing's research shows that we should curb that tendency. When deciding which information to use for non-native listeners, it looks as if quality—selecting content that is appropriate for the individual—matters more than quantity.

Adjusting what you say to match the listener's knowledge and language level is a key classroom skill. As we saw in the 'excursion' episode (Example 4.1), achieving that match may be more difficult for a teacher who is a native teacher of the target language and is unfamiliar with the learners' background. Teachers who share the learners' culture and language have the potential advantage of knowing what information is likely to help.

My study of eavesdroppers' impressions of native–non-native conversation suggests that there is a very fine line between being helpful and being over-helpful, and so we need to be aware of the need to take learners' knowledge into account when deciding how to modify what we tell them. Adult learners will probably be more sensitive on this point than younger ones. When adult students complain about being talked to 'like a child' by someone who has over-elaborated their message, they are in fact reacting to a misjudgement of their experience and intelligence, not their age. For adults, issues of respect and status are important, so they are more aware of speaker-listener accommodation. On the other hand, for younger learners we do need at times to adjust text content to match their knowledge and level of maturity—whether or not they are native speakers (as we saw with the 'Oscar ceremony' news items in Chapter 2). This is not to say that we need not take care when modifying for children and teenagers, but that they may feel less sensitive about it than adults do.

# Effects on learning

The potential advantages of modification summarized so far in this chapter are all short-term, in the sense that the investigations focused on whether various sorts of modification helped learners to understand the current message. But language teachers have to take the longer-term view as well: will interaction contribute to learners' progress? To some extent there is a conflict between these short-term and long-term interests. Modifying everything to make comprehension easier would have the disadvantage of removing the need for learners to confront comprehension problems; it is only by trying to make sense of difficult messages that you become aware of gaps in your knowledge and of the need to extend your command of the language.

In terms of Long's three-step argument (see page 57), research into effects on comprehension is only Step 1. There have been some Step 2 studies, looking at whether successful modifications promote progress in the target language, but exploration of this area is still at an early stage. In fact, there is some dispute among researchers as to whether it is possible to prove a direct link between the comprehension and learning of any particular item. If such a link existed, how would it work? Figure 4.1 shows one possible sketch of the interaction/learning relationship.

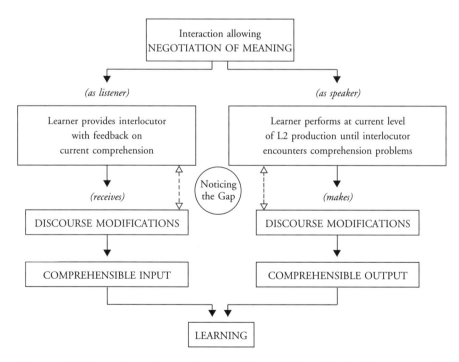

*Figure 4.1: From interaction to learning* (adapted from Shehadeh 1991: 257)

This raises the question of precisely how important interaction is for learning. As you may have noticed, I used Michael Long's phrase earlier when I wrote of interaction *promoting* learning. Applied linguists argue a great deal about the terminology here: does 'promote' mean 'cause' or 'lead to' or 'enable'? Or does it simply mean that interaction 'contributes to' learning? We know that interaction is not essential, because there are situations in which people succeed in learning a language by reading books, without ever having the opportunity to use it, or to hear others using it, in conversation. Craig Chaudron, one of the best known researchers into the input–interaction–learning process, sounds a note of caution about the connections between input, interaction, and learning:

> There is only an inkling of a relationship between comprehensibility or frequency [of input] and learners' progress...
> For the learner to recognize some morphological segment, syntactic rule, or a specific vocabulary item, surely more complex linguistic events and communicative interaction will contribute as much as the simple frequency of occurrence of the item.
> (Chaudron 1988: 163–4)

One 'inkling' as to how learners move from comprehension to learning takes the form of Merrill Swain's Comprehensible Output Hypothesis, outlined in Chapter 2. Example 4.3 below gives a flavour of how learners might be, as Swain says, 'pushed' to greater accuracy in order to get their message through. It comes from a group task involving three intermediate-level students of English (P from Japan, Q from Thailand, and a third who does not speak in this extract). They are working on a pre-writing exercise in which each person has to explain a specialist word to the other two learners. As we join them, learner P is describing a form of 'keyhole' surgery. The teacher has been observing their discussion and now intervenes.

*Example 4.3*

|   |   |   |
|---|---|---|
| P | yeah so we we can + cut gall bladder and sew this injury with some kind of scissor and hotchkiss | |
| Q | hm? | |
| P | + + you know hotchkiss? + hotchkiss? | |
| T | no we don't know that | 5 |
| P | hotchkiss means + + we can use paper | |
| P | scissors? | |
| P | no + clip + uh clip? | |
| T | ah | |
| P | do you know maybe + + many people use like clip with paper | 10 |
| Q | paper clip? | |
| P | yeah paper clip + + or paper hotchkiss + um hotchkiss + + | |

(*takes two sheets of paper and pinches them together with her*
*fingers*) hotchkiss
T    hotchkiss?                                                                          15
P    hotchkiss
T    hotchkiss + + I recognize it as a name but I didn't know
       it was  a clip
Q    I know clip
P    so maybe most people have ever used + + (*finds a stapled*    20
       *set of papers*) ah ah this is hotchkiss
Q    ah st- + um staple
T    staple
P    staple yes + I'm sorry + in Japan hotchkiss (*laughs*) so with
       scissors and with staple through the other two holes + + so    25
       patients can discharge within one week because we only
       open three holes
(observation data)

P is forced to make herself understood by having to respond to her listeners' problems with 'hotchkiss' (line 2). She knows the term from Japan,
where it is in common use, and she has assumed it is also the appropriate
term in English. When it becomes clear that it is not, the three people
negotiate the meaning of the word step by step (lines 3–21), until Q is
eventually able to supply the word that P has been looking for, 'staple',
which the teacher then confirms.

What can we tell from this transcript about the link between interaction
and learning? Is it the first time P has encountered 'staple'? Judging by
the way she reacts to the word, ('staple yes' with falling intonation), it
does seem to be one she has come across before. Otherwise she would
probably have reacted with a confirmation check, 'staple?', or with a
request for repetition or spelling. So it looks as if this negotiation of meaning has resulted in P being reminded of a word that was in fact—at some
level of memory—already part of her English vocabulary.

But can we say that making her meaning comprehensible has helped P to
make the final step in Figure 4.1, to *learn* the word? In other words, has
it fixed 'staple' in P's mind for good? I have referred to Chaudron's argument that there must be other factors, apart from how many times learners encounter an item, that make it memorable. And of course to talk, as
teachers often do, about 'learners' in general is misleading; it disguises the
fact that learners are individual people with individual perceptions, abil-
ities, and memories. Earl Stevick uses the term 'depth' to describe the
extent to which a learner engages with a new item, either intellectually
(e.g. realizing it is important or noticing it is like another word) or
emotionally (e.g. finding it amusing). Stevick argues that we remember

best the items that we find most striking, i.e. engage with at greatest depth.

At this point I am going to indulge in a little speculation, to show how depth of processing might affect an individual's learning. Let's imagine what might have gone through P's mind during the 'hotchkiss' episode. By nature, P is neat, precise, and efficient. She also worries about getting things right. As a doctor, she is professionally trained to look for differences. As a foreigner about to start a medical course in Britain, she is concerned to make a good impression, but is conscious that her spoken English restricts her ability to put herself across. In the classroom episode shown in Example 4.3, she remembers has encountered the word 'staple' in its surgical sense and realizes this is a word she will need in future communication with other doctors. The thought of using the incorrect word 'hotchkiss' in a professional encounter is so embarrassing that it 'marks' the word 'staple' in her mind, as something to remember. So for P, an apparently unimportant mistake—using the wrong word in what is 'only' a classroom exercise—might be all she needs to learn 'staple' once and for all, i.e. for it to be memorable and available when she needs to use it again.

The reason for speculating in this way is to illustrate that in research—as in teaching—it is difficult to be sure whether and when, let alone *how*, a language item has been learnt. We do know that people generally need to encounter and use a new item several times and in different contexts before it 'sticks'. It is hard to *prove* the Comprehensible Output Hypothesis on the evidence of any single interaction; we would need to record a learner's performance over time to be sure that an item is learnt. However, three studies (summarized below) which have examined Swain's hypothesis have shown that interaction on communication tasks does push learners to greater accuracy in the short term.

### Studies 12 and 13: Output in native–non-native talk

One of the first studies to investigate the effect of negotiation of meaning on self-corrections by learners was an experiment carried out by a team led by Teresa Pica (Pica, Holliday, Lewis, and Morgenthaler 1989). They analysed the language produced by 10 Japanese learners of English at the University of Pennsylvania, of pre-intermediate and intermediate level, interacting with 10 native speakers. Each pair was recorded performing three communication tasks: information-gap, where the learner held all the information; jigsaw speaking, where each partner held half the information; and discussion. They found that the production of comprehensible output was affected by two factors. Firstly, it was influenced by the type of signal of comprehension difficulty that the native speaker provided: requests for clarification led to more accurate and fuller self-expression. Secondly, it was influenced by the type of task: native speakers indicated problems most often on the information-gap task, i.e. where the learner held all the information.

A second study followed up this possibility that teachers could help learners to greater accuracy by requesting clarification, rather than by giving explicit correction. Junko Nobuyoshi and Rod Ellis compared the effects of implicit feedback and explicit correction, and did indeed find that clarification requests may also result in better longer-term learning (Nobuyoshi and Ellis 1993). They studied the use of past tense forms by a small group of learners of English at Temple University in Japan. Six students performed two similar tasks a week apart, in which they individually told a picture-based story to their teacher, who had been instructed to respond not with corrections but with various clarification requests (e.g. 'I'm sorry?'). These requests were made when the teacher had either noticed an incorrect past tense form, or genuinely not understood the verb used.

When the teacher responded in this way some learners were able to correct themselves (i.e. even without explicit indication of an error) and also continued to use the correct form a week later on the second task. In other words, there was some evidence that if teachers push learners in the direction of greater accuracy, by indicating that we cannot understand them, we can bring about not only self-correction but also increased accuracy over time, i.e. learning. Of course, the findings of this study are limited by the fact that the period over which 'learning' was measured was just one week—a relatively short time in the context of learning a language.

### Study 14: Output in non-native–non-native conversation
As far as classroom teaching is concerned, Studies 12 and 13 share two limitations: they focused on experimental situations and they featured native–non-native pairs. What about conversation between non-native learners and under classroom conditions? Many teachers (and learners) assume that when learners are working in pairs or small groups, we cannot be sure that the language they produce will be as accurate as when they are interacting individually with us. But research carried out in England found that certain types of pair and group work create conditions for interaction in which learners push each other to speak more comprehensibly and more accurately.

The study was carried out by a Syrian researcher, Ali Shehadeh, at the University of Durham. A total of 35 people participated in his research: eight native speakers and 27 non-native speakers, whose proficiency level ranged from intermediate to post-intermediate and who came from a wide variety of language backgrounds. They worked in pairs on two tasks (information-gap and opinion exchange) and in small groups on a decision-making task (Shehadeh 1991).

Shehadeh's analysis of the task performances showed that, in response to signals of comprehension difficulty from their partner(s), the learners were able to correct their speech to make it more comprehensible. What is more, this happened whether they were talking to native or non-native speakers. Even in learner–learner interaction, the listeners' signals of a comprehension problem led their partners to produce more accurate output eight times out of ten. This is of particular importance, since it suggests that pair and group work in the classroom can result in greater accuracy, provided the task is demanding enough to require real negotiation of meaning.

We have to bear in mind that Shehadeh's study was based in a classroom where most of the learners had no common language other than English, and it would be interesting to see whether the same encouraging results would be found in classrooms where there is a single shared first language.

## Implications for classroom practice

The research reviewed in this section has important practical implications for the way we organize teacher–learner and learner–learner interaction, although as always we have to bear in mind the particular conditions in which they arose.

The two studies of native–non-native interaction, by Pica and colleagues and Nobuyoshi and Ellis, show the possible advantages of teachers asking a learner to clarify what they mean, either when we genuinely have not understood what they have said or when we notice that they have made an error that they might be able to self-correct. Both studies found that prompting learners in this way led to more accurate production at the second attempt. However, this technique has an obvious limitation: asking someone to clarify what they have said can draw their attention to what they *already* know and have got wrong (i.e. a 'slip'), but will not work as a technique for eliciting from students what they *do not yet* know. Errors resulting from genuine gaps in their command of the language will require explicit instruction from the teacher (or other learners), which could come either from pre-teaching or in the form of feedback during or after an activity. I will come back to this point in Chapter 6.

Shehadeh's findings are further evidence of the potential value of learner–learner interaction, especially in large classes. He was able to show that learners modified their output (correcting errors of pronunciation, grammar, or vocabulary), even when they were talking to another non-native speaker, and without the intervention of the teacher. Shehadeh has added one more contribution to a series of findings that emphasize the potential value of group work. Of course, group work is not without its problems, which can be practical (such as physical organization and keeping 'noise' to an acceptable level), or cultural, having to do with local beliefs about the roles of learners and teachers. But from the point of view of encouraging interaction and negotiation of meaning, there are plenty of reasons for believing that group work brings positive benefits. In Chapter 6 I will discuss some of the practicalities of setting up pair and group work in ways that lead to purposeful interaction.

# Summary

In this chapter I have summarized some of the evidence that the adjustments typically made for the intended benefit of listeners *do* help them to achieve greater levels of comprehension, measured in a variety of ways. Some researchers have compared the potential benefits of adopting one type of modification rather than another, and it appears that interaction offers the most effective route to understanding. In practice, teachers are likely to combine a number of different modification tactics—for example, checking comprehension (interaction modification) and then repeating problematic words more slowly and clearly (input modification) to give the learners a second chance to understand.

The evidence from currently available research on discourse modifications for language learners could be summarized as follows:

– modification of input helps
– modification of interaction helps more
– modifications of information choice can hinder.

The clear message from a variety of classroom experiments is that the opportunity to obtain discourse modifications by active negotiation of meaning through interaction with other speakers (teacher and/or learners) helps students to solve communication problems and provides a platform for learning. In Part Two of this book I explore the implications of an interaction-orientated approach for the teaching of the four traditional skills.

## *Suggestions for further reading*

### *Input, interaction, and learning*
**Gass, S.** and **C. Madden.** (eds.). 1985. *Input in Second Language Acquisition.* Rowley, Mass.: Newbury House. This contains a number of useful papers on the comprehension–learning connection, in particular those by Hawkins (1985), Swain (1985), and Long (1985).

### Affective dimension of L2 learning

**Harder, P.** 1981. 'Discourse as self-expression: On the reduced personality of the second-language learner'. *Applied Linguistics* 1/3: 262–70. Unusually for an academic paper, this is written to amuse as well as to inform. It deals with the frustrations of feeling 'less than' yourself when speaking a foreign language, and is a useful reminder that learners are people too.

### Negotiation

**Pica, T.** 1994. 'Research on negotiation: What does it reveal about second-language learning conditions, processes, and outcomes?' *Language Learning* 44/3: 493–527. In this recent survey Teresa Pica shows that negotiation seems to help some aspects of language learning more than others. She discusses possible areas for future research, such as ways of supporting negotiation-orientated tasks with form-focused teaching.

## Research studies mentioned in this chapter

### Input
### Study 1: Highlighting the topic

**Chaudron, C.** 1983. 'Simplification of input: topic reinstatements and their effects on L2 learners' recognition and recall.' *TESOL Quarterly* 17/3: 437–58.

### Study 2: Repetition

**Cervantes, R.** 1983. 'Say it Again, Sam: The Effect of Exact Repetition on Listening Comprehension.' Term paper, University of Hawaii at Manoa.

### Study 3: Rate of speaking

**Kelch, K.** 1985. 'Modified input as an aid to comprehension.' *Studies in Second Language Acquisition* 7/1: 81–90.

### Study 4: Rate of speaking

**Griffiths, R.** 1990. 'Speech rate and NNS comprehension: a preliminary study'. *Language Learning* 40/3: 311–36.

### Study 5: Syntactic simplification

**Cervantes, R.** and **G. Gainer.** 1992. 'The effects of syntactic simplification and repetition on listening comprehension.' *TESOL Quarterly* 26/4: 767–70.

### Study 6: Elaboration

**Chiang, C. S.** and **P. Dunkel.** 1992. 'The effect of speech modification, prior knowledge and listening proficiency on EFL lecture learning.' *TESOL Quarterly* 26/2: 345–74.

*Interaction*
*Study 7: Interaction versus input*
**Pica T., R. Young,** and **C. Doughty.** 1987. 'The impact of interaction on comprehension'. *TESOL Quarterly* 21/4: 737–58.

*Study 8: Observing interaction*
**Lynch, A.** 1988a. 'Grading Foreign Language Listening Comprehension Materials: the Use of Naturally Modified Interaction'. Ph.D. dissertation, University of Edinburgh, Scotland.

*Study 9: Participating versus observing*
**Pica, T.** 1991. 'Classroom interaction, negotiation and comprehension: redefining relationships'. *System* 19/4: 437–52.

*Information choice*
*Study 10: Effects on comprehension*
**Derwing, T.** 1989. 'Information type and its relation to nonnative speaker comprehension.' *Language Learning* 39/2: 157–73.

*Study 11: Effects on learners' perceptions*
**Lynch, A.** 1988b. 'Speaking up or talking down: foreign learners' reactions to teacher talk.' *ELT Journal* 42/2: 109–16.

*Output and learning*
*Study 12: Output in native–non-native talk*
**Pica, T., L. Holliday, N. Lewis,** and **L. Morgenthaler.** 1989. 'Comprehensible output as an outcome of linguistic demands on the learner'. *Studies in Second Language Acquisition* 11/1: 63–90.

*Study 13: Output in teacher–learner talk*
**Nobuyoshi, J.** and **R. Ellis.** 1993. 'Focused communication tasks and second language acquisition.' *ELT Journal* 47/3: 203–10.

*Study 14: Output in learner–learner talk*
**Shehadeh, A.** 1991. 'Comprehension and Performance in Second Language Acquisition: A Study of Second Language Learners' Production of Modified Comprehensible Output.' Ph.D. dissertation. University of Durham, England.

# PART TWO

## Classroom applications— interaction-based teaching

# INTRODUCTION

In Part One I considered ways in which people negotiate their way through the difficulties that can naturally arise in the course of a conversation. Looking at communication in this way tends to highlight comprehension problems as obstacles. In the short term, they are. But from the longer-term perspective, comprehension problems are vital opportunities for learning. If learners encountered no difficulties of understanding, they would not need to go beyond their current level. It is by having to cope with a problem—either in understanding someone else or in expressing themselves—that they may notice the gap and may learn the missing item.

But making progress in a language depends on more than accumulating new knowledge in the form of 'items' of vocabulary or grammar. Learners need to develop fluency in using these items in communication and it is here that classroom practice in the four traditional skills plays an important part. It helps them to become more comfortable in the language, to find the right words or meanings more quickly. In Part Two of this book I present ways in which skills practice can incorporate activities based on the principles drawn from interaction research. I am not claiming that *all* skills teaching can be exclusively based on interactive principles, but that we should find a place for it in our repertoire of techniques for teaching listening, speaking, reading, and writing.

# 5 TEACHING LISTENING

In this chapter I suggest ways of teaching listening that will help learners to resolve comprehension problems. This includes developing their confidence in their ability to understand as well as their competence in listening. I demonstrate alternative ways of grading the learners' experience of listening—by text, by task, and by interaction. The opening Activity reviews what spoken language looks and sounds like.

## *Activity*

### Spoken language

Below is an extract from an English language course for German intermediate-level learners. It features a German teenager, Klaus, who is staying in the home of the West family in Britain. In this scene, Klaus notices the Wests' son Tom looking at an atlas, and the conversation turns to geography. How typical do you think the dialogue is of the sort of spontaneous conversation we have looked at in Part One?

*Example 5.1*

| | |
|---|---|
| Mr West | *(to Klaus)* Yes, your frontiers have changed constantly during the last centuries. During that period your country has often varied in size. Sometimes it was smaller, sometimes larger. All the worst and longest European wars have directly affected Germany, especially the last, from 1939 to 1945. |
| Mrs West | I wonder why your country has been involved in almost every war on the Continent. |
| Klaus | The reason for this is its geographic position, I think. Germany is in the middle of Europe and has more bordering states than any other country. Before the last war Germany had ten neighbours. The more neighbours a country has, the greater is the danger of war. You British are luckier than we are. You're in the best position |

|          | geographically. You live on an island and you have no neighbours nearer than France, and that is 21 miles away across the Channel at the nearest point. |
|----------|---|
| **Tom** | Just a minute! We have a neighbour nearer than that: Ireland. |
| **Klaus** | Well, Ireland has never given you any trouble. |
| **Tom** | That's quite wrong. The Irish Republic or Eire, as it is now called, fought hard for its independence, and even now it would like to take over Northern Ireland as well. But Northern Ireland, like England, Scotland and Wales, is part of the United Kingdom. |
| **Mrs West** | Let's have no more talk about politics. Let's talk about the weather instead. I've always wondered why we have less snow in the winter than you in Germany, although we're further north. |

(*Englisch für berufsbildende Schulen* 1975: 166, quoted in Schwerdtfeger 1983: 152–3)

That 'dialogue' bears little resemblance to the natural give-and-take of real interaction. The writer has included a few features of spoken English, such as the reduced forms 'you're', 'that's', and 'I've', and expressions like 'just a minute' and 'well'. But these are cosmetic. The complex and precise sentences the characters produce are more typical of edited writing than of unplanned speech. Ironically, the longest and most complex speaking turn is one produced by Klaus—who seems to be strangely word-perfect for someone who is staying with a British family to improve his English!

Example 5.1 illustrates the risks of assuming that speech is simply a spoken form of writing. Both the forms of language used and the density of the information in the dialogue are quite different from the typical features of real conversation—especially between native and non-native speakers, as that dialogue was supposed to be. So the listening materials presented to learners as samples of interaction ought to reflect the natural patterns of negotiation by which listener and speaker work their way towards mutual understanding.

# Problem-solving strategies

When the learner becomes aware of a listening problem, it may be due to a gap in the input (e.g. *not hearing* part of an utterance because of traffic noise) or in their grammar or vocabulary (e.g. *not knowing* the meaning of a key word). It could also be due to affective factors, such as *not being interested* in the topic, or to attention problems, such as *thinking about something else*. Even if they realize that the cause of their difficulty is a gap in their own knowledge, some learners may assume it is up to the speaker (often the teacher) to do something to bridge the gap. Successful listeners are those who take active steps to sort out listening problems. For example, they monitor their comprehension as they listen ('Have I understood that last bit?') and they assess how adequate the speaker's message is ('Has she given me clear enough information?').

When these competent listeners encounter a major problem in understanding, they adopt an appropriate strategy to resolve it. The Danish applied linguist Claus Færch divided listening strategies into two types: *psycholinguistic* and *behavioural* (Færch 1981). *Psycholinguistic* strategies are unseen actions 'in the head'. They involve the listener's conscious use of their personal 'comprehension resources', described in Chapter 2 (pages 20–22): for example, the listener might exploit contextual clues and background knowledge, or guess at meaning on the basis of a word's structure. I will be referring to these as *internal* strategies.

*Behavioural* strategies, on the other hand, are visible actions 'in the world'. They rely on negotiation with the speaker—making general requests ('I don't understand'), specific requests ('What does X mean?') or admitting ignorance ('I don't know that word'). To emphasize the extent to which these strategies depend on collaboration with the other person or people, I will call them *interactive* strategies.

A basic problem for the teaching of listening is that learners' internal activity is largely unobservable. This has two disadvantages in the classroom: (1) it is difficult for teachers to judge how much their students are understanding, and (2) it is difficult for each student to know how well they are coping compared with the other listeners.

## *Paused listening tasks*

One way of getting learners to interpret in a public way what is normally hidden is to use paused listening tasks. These are listening activities in which the teacher stops the tape (or pauses in speaking), and asks the learners to compare their evolving interpretations of what the text is about. Research suggests that when trying to understand a foreign language we deal with some problems less flexibly than we would in our own language. The German researcher Gabriele Kasper (1984) compared the way that different listeners coped when a speaker changed topic in the course of a conversation. She found that non-native listeners tended to form an initial topic interpretation (or 'frame') and stick to it. Native listeners were better at recognizing when they had made a mistake about the topic and were more prepared to construct a new interpretation (Kasper 1984).

The text below is one I use to encourage learners of English to talk about their current *mental model* (internal picture) of a message. It is based on a real-life conversation between two of my colleagues, which I overheard and found hard to follow. I play it in five segments, each consisting of a pair of speaking turns by A and B.

*Example 5.2*
>    **A**   What's it like, then?
>    **B**   Not bad. It's got a good short menu, which saves quite a bit of time.
>    *STOP*
>    **A**   It doesn't have a mouse does it?
>    **B**   No, not at that price.
>    *STOP*
>    **A**   Anything else special?
>    **B**   Well, it's got a thing to stop you having to worry about widows and orphans.
>    *STOP*
>    **A**   So you're happy with it, then?
>    **B**   So far, yes.
>    *STOP*
>    **A**   And did you get the 512 in the end?
>    **B**   No, the 256.
>    *STOP*

After each segment I ask the listeners to write down (1) what they believe the topic is, and (2) which word or phrase makes them think so. They are allowed to modify, abandon, or retain their interpretation at each stopping point. In effect they produce a 'commentary' on their process of understanding the conversation. Some learners write down a different topic at each of the five stopping points; others keep to one throughout. Table 5.1 shows commentaries written by three listeners (two teachers of English and one of their intermediate-level students) who were played a recording of Example 5.2.

You will probably find it difficult to tell which listener was the learner of English; in fact, it was listener A. From her commentary it seems she had no doubt at any stage that the two people were talking about computers. As it happens, she had a degree in artificial intelligence and was able to use both her knowledge of English and her background knowledge to interpret the message. Although teachers B and F had a native command of the language, they were confused by 'menu', 'mouse', and 'widows and orphans'. But in the end they both reached the correct solution, though for different reasons: F relied solely on the fact that the numbers sounded like a model of computer; B also remembered at the final stopping point that 'menu' was a term she had heard other people use when talking about computers.

| Stop | Listener A | Listener B | Listener F |
|---|---|---|---|
| 1 *Topic* | COMPUTERS | RESTAURANT | FAST-FOOD RESTAURANT |
| *Reason* | 'menu' | 'menu' | – |
| 2 *Topic* | COMPUTERS | RESTAURANT? | I don't understand this! |
| *Reason* | 'mouse' | but why 'mouse'? | – |
| 3 *Topic* | COMPUTERS | CHARITY COFFEE BAR | Still cannot make sense of it |
| *Reason* | 'widows and orphans' | 'widows and orphans' | |
| 4 *Topic* | COMPUTERS | SOMETHING A HAS BOUGHT | BOAT? |
| *Reason* | 'happy with it' | – | – |
| 5 *Topic* | DEFINITELY COMPUTERS | COMPUTERS | COMPUTER? |
| *Reason* | – | numbers and 'menu' | By elimination —the numbers |

(Lynch 1987)

*Table 5.1: Commentaries on paused listening*

It is only too easy to get dispirited when listening to a language of which you have a limited knowledge. The advantage of paused listening tasks is that they do not penalize the learners for being unsure how right they are. When I show students the commentaries of listeners A, B, and F, it encourages them to have a little more faith in their own interpretations when they see that native speakers, too, can take time to work out what the topic is.

Even in first language listening, researchers have found that some people are 'listener-blamers': when they do not understand what is said to them, they assume it is their fault, even when the speaker's message is actually vague or ambiguous. Some educational cultures tend to make children 'listener-blamers' by emphasizing the role of the teacher as possessor of knowledge and authority figure. This has the effect of discouraging pupil-to-teacher questioning and so when studying a foreign language, learners from these cultures may be reluctant to ask the speaker for clarification (Pica 1987; Rost and Ross 1991). Paused listening tasks can help to show learners that comprehension is gradual and that they are not unusual if they cannot reach a definitive interpretation straight away.

Paused listening is particularly effective when practised on video material, where you can stop at a suitable point and ask the learners to report what they have understood so far, or to use visual clues to predict what is about to happen. But paused listening tasks need not be based on recorded material. You can also pause when telling a story off the cuff or when reading out a text.

## Types of listening

Internal and interactive strategies may be used together, but of course there are some situations in which it is simply not possible to use interactive strategies: when listening is a one-way event where the listener has no chance to ask for help from the speaker. Most of the examples I have used in this book so far occurred in two-way conversations, in which the listeners had the opportunity to ask for help from the speaker when they needed to. However, in many everyday situations listening is one-way communication: the listener has no chance to respond to what is said and may be remote from the speaker, for example, when listening to the radio or watching television.

The question of whether the listener is *able* to intervene to get help also raises the issue of whether they feel *entitled* to do. We have to bear in mind that the listener may have different rights (or responsibilities) in different situations. There are some face-to-face situations where the listener is physically able to respond but is not expected to, such as in the public gallery of a courtroom; or where the listener is permitted to respond only in limited ways, such as at religious ceremonies. One analysis (McGregor 1986) proposes a range of five listener roles:

*Participant:* someone who is being spoken to and has the same speaking rights as others present

*Addressee:* someone who is being spoken to but has limited rights to speak

*Auditor:* someone who is being spoken to but is not expected to respond

*Overhearer:* someone who is not being spoken to and has no right to speak

*Judge:* someone who is not being spoken to but is required to evaluate the speaker or the message

(adapted from Rost 1990: 5)

That classification was intended to apply to roles in real-life listening.

When it comes to the roles learners are asked to play in the classroom, things become more complicated. When a teacher uses recorded listening comprehension material, the learners' role may be different from that of the original listener. For example, the teacher may ask them to listen to an informal conversation. The listener in the conversation was a participant; in the classroom the learners adopt the role of overhearers (answering questions on the content of what was said) or judges (assessing the emotions of the two speakers).

To some extent these issues of situation and role are interconnected, as the examples in Table 5.2 show.

|  | participant | addressee | auditor | overhearer | judge |
|---|---|---|---|---|---|
| *one-way* |  | listening to a telephone answering machine | listening to a radio phone-in | hearing someone leaving a telephone message | a juror listening to a witness in a court |
| *two-way* | holding an informal conversation | listening to a lecture | listening to a debate between politicians | listening to other people's conversation | (an inspector) watching a school lesson |

*Table 5.2: Situation and role in listening*

As teachers, our expectations about what is 'effective listening' need to vary with the particular demands of the situation. We should certainly not expect learners of a language to achieve a more complete or more precise understanding than a competent native listener would in that situation.

Whatever the precise role, an effective listener is actively involved, even if that involvement takes the form of internal, hidden action. To emphasize the contribution the listener makes to the successful reception of a message, writers on the comprehension process often use the expression '*making* sense' to refer to what the listener (or reader) does. This takes us back to the analogy between comprehension and a do-it-yourself furniture kit, mentioned in Chapter 2: the listener/reader assembles meaning from the clues offered by the speaker/writer.

# Grading

In trying to help our students to make sense, we have a number of techniques at our disposal. Paused listening tasks such as the one illustrated earlier do not make the text itself easier; what they do is make the learners feel more relaxed about their efforts to understand it. They aim to build confidence by getting a learner used to having a rough initial picture of what the speaker means, and gradually refining that picture as more information comes in.

Another approach to making success in listening more likely is to grade the learners' experience of the spoken language, from more straightforward to more complex. Traditionally, the grading of classroom listening activities has been based on two broad options: to grade the *text* or grade the *task*. Each of these options can be subdivided, as shown in Figure 5.1.

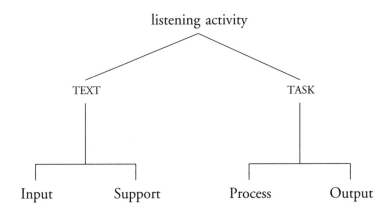

*Figure 5.1: Conventional options in grading listening*

The text can be made easier by adjusting the input itself, or the support material. *Input* can be *pre-modified*, for example by preparing a script that restricts the number of unfamiliar items. Alternatively a recording can be *post-modified*, e.g. by editing out faster or more complex passages, in order to leave easier listening extracts for students to work on. Grading through *Support* might involve providing additional help in the form of materials to accompany the listening passage itself, such as a list of vocabulary which the students work through before hearing the text.

On the Task side of the diagram, we can adjust aspects of process or output. *Process* has to do with listening purpose: e.g. whether you ask the learners to pick out the key points, to identify the current topic of conversation, or to tell where a speaker is from by their accent. *Output* can be adjusted through the physical product required of the learner in order to demonstrate that they have performed the task satisfactorily: asking learners for a non-verbal response such as matching or ticking, or answering questions in their first language, would tend to make this aspect of the task easier.

Let's take a practical example of what is in real life a one-way listening situation, a radio weather forecast, and see how it might be graded in those four ways.

*Example 5.3*

Good morning. A brighter day for eastern regions but showers are gathering in the west and they'll be supported by the approach of low pressure. Today it's a frosty start in many places with icy roads very likely in the next couple of hours or so in south-east, central southern England, the Midlands and East Anglia, along with north-east England and eastern Scotland; a dry and fairly bright morning, quite a bit of sunshine and the temperature picking up to around 4 or 5 degrees, about 40 Fahrenheit. It'll turn cloudy this afternoon with showers marching across from the west, these helped along by a freshening south-westerly wind. The showers probably clustering together to give some lengthy spells of rain or sleet later this afternoon and evening, and probably turning to snow in places, more especially in the north and over high ground in the south.

Now the forecast for western parts, for the Channel Islands and south-west England, Wales, the Isle of Man and north-west England, along with Northern Ireland and western Scotland. Some bright spells this morning but there are showers about already er some thunder around in western Scotland and er in the during the morning in these western regions it's going to turn generally cloudier er showers probably leading into a longer spell of rain or sleet with some snow on the hills during this afternoon probably clearing up towards evening but soon freezing after dusk. Highest temperatures mostly around 4 or 5 degrees, close to 40 Fahrenheit, perhaps a bit higher near south-western coasts. And the south-westerly wind, that's going to be quite strong for a time er during this morning and early afternoon, probably easing off and turning more westerly again as we go towards evening.

And looking ahead at the prospects during the next couple of days there's certainly a wintry look to the weather during tomorrow and Thursday er low pressure slipping southward across us and bringing mainly cloudy weather with sleet or snow in places and opening the door for some very cold easterly winds er during later on Wednesday and Thursday, and night frost in many places. And that's the forecast.

(total: 2 minutes)

Alternatives for grading the difficulty of classroom activities based on that forecast include the following:

***Grading the text: Input***     Possible modifications to the input are: to record a simplified version in which some less familiar expressions (e.g. 'bright spells') are replaced with more frequent ones (e.g. 'sunny periods'); to reduce the length of the text by playing only the first paragraph; to keep the text as it is but to pause after each sentence; to take out some of the references to places (East Anglia, Isle of Man, Channel Islands) that the learners may not know.

***Grading the text: Support***     You could give learners a list of weather vocabulary: 'snow, sleet, hail, ice, frost'. The list might include only words mentioned in the forecast, or it could have additional items (depending on the nature of the task—see 'Output' below). You could provide a map of the British Isles with the relevant regional names marked. You could give them a transcript of the recording with blanks for them to complete as they listen.

***Grading the task: Process***     The level of complexity of the task can be adjusted in various ways in order to match your students' level. For example, a relatively simple task would be to answer the question *What time of year is it?* (notice how many potential clues there are for them to pick up as they listen). You could ask them to decide whether, having heard about the weather, they would rather visit somewhere indoors like a museum, or outdoors like a safari park. An example of a much more difficult task would be to identify as many place names as they can (or weather words, or expressions meaning *approximately*).

***Grading the task: Output***     Any of the Process elements could be made easier by allowing the learners to answer in their first language, or asking them to choose from items (places, weather words, etc.) in a list, rather than starting with a blank sheet of paper.

So there are plenty of ways of reducing or increasing the level of comprehension difficulty. But both text-based and task-based methods of grading have their disadvantages. Grading the text raises the complex question of how to assess the level of vocabulary. The fact that a particular item is unusual does not necessarily mean that, in the context of a particular message, it will be hard to understand. So it is hard to predict which new items are going to be problematic for a particular learner in a specific listening text. The best way to assess text difficulty is to ask learners to try it out.

Grading the task can have the disadvantage of leading to a conflict of expectations—between what the teacher or materials writer expects of the students and what they expect of themselves. Adult elementary-level students sometimes express frustration at being able to answer what they regard as the over-simple questions they are asked in comprehension materials (e.g. to say how many speakers are taking part in a conversation), which they can do without having understood much of the text.

The variety of things we can do to exploit a sample of real language should not make us lose sight of the real-life purpose for which someone would actually listen to a spoken text. But that has to be kept as a goal to aim for rather than something we should expect to achieve, especially with learners at lower levels. Of the possible activities I listed for Example 5.3, probably the most lifelike task is the one that asks learners to decide what sort of trip to make, depending on the weather. It might be possible for quite low-level listeners to answer that in this case, since they might well notice the low temperatures mentioned, and work out that it was not a good day for going outside. So realistic listening purposes with unmodified texts are feasible for elementary-level students, provided the content of the text allows it.

## *Interaction-based grading*

A radio weather forecast is an example of real-life one-way listening. The normal way of using one in the classroom is to get the learners to listen silently while the whole passage is played (or read aloud). Their response is limited to answering questions or completing some sort of task devised by the teacher—or in many cases by a materials writer remote from the learning situation. In one-way tasks, listeners exert no direct influence over what the speaker says and how they say it. The text is not negotiable.

However, two-way situations where listeners are able to both hear and respond require rather different treatment in the classroom; we need to devise listening activities that focus on interactive listening strategies, in order to prepare learners for active negotiation of meaning. I am going to describe two such activities here. The first involves what I call *second-hand negotiation*, whereby the learners listen to a conversation (i.e. what was originally a two-way text) and can take advantage of the negotiation of meaning between listener and speaker. The second practises *indirect negotiation*: the learners hear a one-way text (a recorded set of instructions) and can respond by getting clarification, but from the teacher not the original speaker.

### Second-hand negotiation

This technique is based on the research described under Study 8 in Chapter 4. It involves recording two people performing an information-gap task, one of whom is a non-native speaker. Instead of simplifying the spoken text by pre-modifying it or post-modifying it, I exploit the *on-line modifications*, the changes negotiated by listener and speaker during the task itself.

The 'ingredients' for the recording are: a native or fluent speaker of the target language, such as a teaching colleague (or yourself); an audio- or video-recorder; a learner at roughly the same level as the group with whom you plan to use the material. However, it is not simply a matter of turning on the recorder and telling the two people to talk. To ensure that their interaction contains the sort of adjustments needed for comprehensibility, the listener needs to have some concrete task to achieve, such as sequencing or numbering items on a list, completing a grid, etc. The speaker is more likely to modify any difficult parts of the message if the listener needs to understand them for a specific reason.

It is also essential to encourage the listener to tell the speaker when problems occur, so that the speaker knows when to make modifications for comprehension. This should create the right conditions for the speaker to adjust their message for the benefit of the original listener (and therefore also of the learners listening to the recording in class).

This technique offers a do-it-yourself solution to the basic problem that teachers face in many parts of the world: lack of easy access to English language broadcasts or to commercial listening materials. The reason for using material recorded in this way is as a means to an end: to show learners what negotiation of meaning sounds and looks like. I use this sort of recording first as comprehension material, with the learners completing the same task as the original listener. On a second hearing I ask them to look for the ways in which the listener and speaker negotiated their way out of their communication problems. This leads on to speaking tasks in which the learners put into practice the tactics they have heard the two partners use on tape. I will be dealing with this area in more detail in Chapter 6.

### Indirect negotiation

As I mentioned earlier, task-based grading includes adjusting two aspects of listening tasks: process and output. The usual way to grade process is in terms of the level of comprehension required of the listener. The activity I am going to present in this section involves changing the learners' role from overhearers to participants. In real conversation this is the role we normally assume; being a participant gives us the opportunity to use both the interactive and the internal strategies that Claus Færch described.

The interaction research reported in Chapter 4 shows that the effective use of interactive negotiation is one of the things that differentiate successful listeners from less successful ones. The videotaped narratives described in the previous section give learners the benefits of negotiation

at *second hand*, carried out on their behalf by the partners in the recordings. A further step towards live negotiation is to develop listening tasks
that encourage learners to interact with a recorded text. At first sight the
idea of 'interaction' with a cassette may seem odd, but I will describe some
materials in which grading is achieved not by adjusting the text in advance,
but by giving the learners the chance to get help with their current listening problem.

The materials were originally designed to improve the first language
listening skills of secondary pupils in Scotland (for details, see Anderson
and Lynch 1988). The learners hear various types of recorded text—
descriptions of places, instructions for drawing diagrams, and people's personal stories. As they listen, they complete a task sheet. Some recorded
passages were scripted and include deliberate ambiguities and unclear references, of the sort that often occur in natural speech. Some learners are
told that when they have difficulty understanding any part of the recording, they are to ask the teacher to stop the tape. In groups, they then con-
sult and have to agree on one of four 'routes' to clarification. They can
choose to:

1 hear the problematic section again
2 see whether the next part of the text will help
3 ask the teacher for additional information
4 see whether anyone has a satisfactory solution that makes it unneces-
  sary to take any of routes 1–3.

The reason for designing these listening materials to encourage 'indirect'
negotiation was precisely because some of the young Scottish pupils they
were written for were known to lack confidence in asking teachers for help
(and not only in English classes). Allowing them to interrupt a recorded
message and deciding in what way it was inadequate was intended to be
a stepping stone towards gaining enough confidence to interrupt the
teacher. (The teachers of other subjects did indeed notice that the pupils
started to ask many more questions in their lessons, but that is another
story!)

Example 5.4 shows a group of adult learners on a general English course
at intermediate level, working on one of the Scottish tasks, in which they
are following a set of recorded instructions and updating a map of a town
centre. The listeners' version of the map is shown below; it is slightly different from the one being described by the speaker on tape.

At the point where we join them, they have just heard the instruction
'Cosmos Holidays, Plush Carpets, and Brown's have all gone and instead
there's just one store. So cross them out and write in the word
"Supermarket" across all three shops'. The listeners' map shows the type

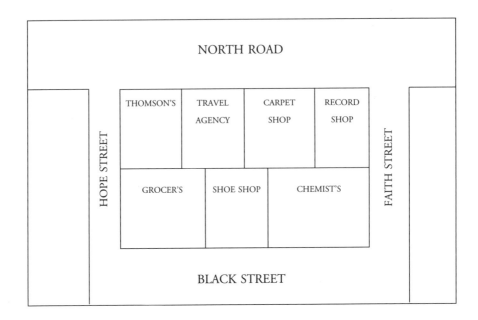

*Figure 5.2: Map of town centre* (from Scottish Education Department 1984)

of shop that used to operate in the town centre, but does not mention them by name. So the learners have asked the teacher to stop the tape; after some discussion it becomes clear that all but one of the group think they need to ask the teacher for more information. Only learner G (Gabriela) is not convinced that they require more.

***Example 5.4***

    T  I suspect that Gabriela thinks she doesn't need any information + is that right?

    G  no

    T  you don't need any more information + would you all agree with that?

    Ss  no

    T  well ask Gabriela first and see if she can persuade you that you don't + if you do you can ask me

    G  he said + um + that the carpet shop is closed

    F  yes I know

    G  and then he mentioned two names

    Ss  yes

    G  first must be the name of the travel agency

    Ss  yes

    G  and the other must be the record shop

    F  why?

    K  uhuh

G   because Thomson's is a name
K   but it could also be shoe shop down + perhaps there is a super-
      market like this *(shows a T-shape on his map)*
G   no + it's in North Road
Ss  yes *(hubbub)*
A   because Thomson's is a name it's not a
G   a sort
A   a kind of shop + he would have telled 'electronic shop'
G   that's right
T   are you all convinced?
(observation data)

From this point on, group discussion—prompted by the teacher—
gradually works towards the selection of the best strategy. Later in the discussion, *en route* to their decision, the learners discuss and reject various
possibilities: 'she would have said . . .', 'yes but if she talked about . . .',
and 'it can also be the shoe shop'. Once they have persuaded Gabriela
that they do need to ask the teacher for clarifying information, they discuss what sort of information would help them. Various members of the
group suggest asking whether there are two ways into the new shop, what
sort of shops occupy the site of the supermarket on their map, the name
of the owner of the record shop. In the end they agree to ask the teacher
what kind of shop Brown's is. His answer resolves the ambiguity and they
can then carry on to the next part of the recording.

Comparisons of performances by native and non-native listeners on this
sort of indirect negotiation task have shown great similarities between the
two groups of listener (Anderson and Lynch 1988; Lynch 1991). The way
the tasks are designed means that, with varying amounts of discussion and
questioning, listeners at very different levels of English (from native to elementary) are able to complete the comprehension task successfully. As the
listeners become more familiar with what is expected of them, the
teachers' participation in the decision-making tends to decrease over the
series of tasks—even though the later ones are designed to be more difficult.

What makes these tasks manageable, even for the weakest listeners, is the
opportunity to discuss current difficulties and the absence of time pressure. By allowing them freedom in these two aspects of the listening
process, the task is made accessible to everyone. The main difference is
that elementary-level groups take longer than more advanced ones. The
learners gain experience not just in listening to realistic spoken English
but also in identifying appropriate strategies to tackle specific problems.

This map task is an almost literal version of the 'pushdown' mentioned
in Chapter 1 (see page 9). Any listener can ask for the pause button to
be pressed, while the group decide whether there really is a problem and,

if so, how best to resolve it. It encourages learners to make conscious and explicit decisions about whether difficulties in spoken information can be resolved by internal strategies (e.g. inference or concentrating on the next part of the message) or by interactive strategies, such as asking for repetition. Strategically successful listeners cope with a problem by deciding on the appropriate route to a solution and then putting a plan into effective action. Tasks such as the town centre map activity help learners to have the confidence to do that.

The aim of using recordings in this way is to encourage weaker listeners to ask for more help from the teacher and so to get the modifications they need. Having experienced second-hand and indirect negotiation, learners should be more prepared to engage in *direct* negotiation of meaning with the teacher. Of course I recognize that this suggestion makes certain cultural assumptions about what is desirable behaviour in class. In some educational contexts learners are expected to play a relatively passive role, awaiting *instruction from* the teacher rather than *interaction with* the teacher. So teachers should look for locally appropriate solutions to the problem of increasing learners' chances of understanding, by giving them the opportunity to ask for clarification when they need it. We now have evidence, from the sort of research I discussed in Chapter 4, that negotiation of meaning between learners and teacher is beneficial; we should be looking for ways of making it acceptable.

# Summary

In this chapter I have discussed ways of helping learners towards interactive negotiation through listening practice based on recorded messages. Paused listening tasks provide a platform for comparing their interpretations of spoken messages. In second-hand negotiation tasks, the presence of an original listener 'obliges' the speaker to adjust to the level of that partner, which assists learners watching or listening to the recording in the classroom. In the case of the town centre materials, the recorded text itself was not modified—in fact, it was made intentionally difficult, even for pupils listening in their first language. But the teaching procedure gave the listeners the chance to intervene and negotiate with the speaker indirectly, via the teacher.

The key to successful use of both internal and interactive strategies is *flexibility*, which comes from a combination of adequate command of the language and confidence from practice in dealing with comprehension problems. The next step towards full negotiation is to create tasks that allow full two-way communication, where learners interact with a live speaker. It is to this type of classroom task that we turn in Chapter 6.

## *Suggestions for further reading*

### *Teaching listening*

**Brown, G.** 1990. *Listening to Spoken English* (2nd edition). London: Longman. This book explains in detail the features of spoken English that cause problems for non-native listeners. The final chapter is a useful discussion of how to get learners used to natural speech.

**Rost, M.** 1990. *Listening in Language Learning.* London: Longman. The most comprehensive book on the role of listening. Rost deals with both the social and psychological sides of listening. Chapters 6 and 7 deal with classroom teaching and testing.

### *Grading*

**Anderson, A.** and **T. Lynch.** 1988. *Listening.* Oxford: Oxford University Press. Chapters 4 and 6 cover grading of listening, both in the mother tongue and in foreign languages. Chapter 7 illustrates the graded Scottish project materials (referred to in this book) for interactive listening, and assesses their effects.

**Nunan, D.** 1989. *Designing Tasks for the Communicative Classroom.* Cambridge: Cambridge University Press. Nunan explores the varied factors to take into account when assessing the difficulty of classroom materials and tasks, and applies them to the teaching of all four skills. Includes plenty of examples.

# 6 TEACHING SPEAKING

Listening and reading are useful sources of experience, but active practice in—and feedback on—speaking and writing the target language is essential for faster progress. In the classroom, 'speaking' can cover a wide range of oral activities, from genuine interaction (i.e. actually talking to someone about something) to repetition drills. The Activity below compares two ways in which learners may be involved in speaking.

## *Activity*

### Questions in class

These classroom extracts both feature contributions by teacher and learners. I would like you to pay particular attention to the use of questions (underlined). Look for differences between the patterns of questioning: Who asks whom? What sort of questions get asked? What is the response?

The first sequence comes from a primary school English lesson, where the teacher is dealing with an exercise in the class's textbook on 'a' or 'an'.

*Example 6.1*

| | |
|---|---|
| Teacher | <u>Now do we say 'a old man'?</u> |
| Chorus | No. |
| Teacher | No we don't say 'a old man'. You know the word 'an', it's A-N and A-N . . . <u>A is what?</u> A is a vowel, it's a vowel, so we say 'an old man'. O also . . . O is the beginning of the word, O is a vowel, so we say 'an old man' not 'a old man'. <u>You understand, boys?</u> |
| Chorus | Yes. |
| Teacher | Now the second word is 'sum'. Look for the right word in column B. <u>What do you add to the word 'sum'?</u> Yes, Usman. Are you . . . you have to hold your reading book so that you get the right answer. |
| Usman | Today's sum it is easy. |

| | |
|---|---|
| **Teacher** | No. Just give the one word from column B, just one word. |
| **Usman** | 'Easy'. |
| **Teacher** | 'Easy'. <u>Is he correct?</u> |
| **Chorus** | Yes. |
| **Teacher** | <u>Is he correct?</u> |
| **Chorus** | No. |
| **Teacher** | No, you are not sure. <u>Is he correct?</u> He says 'easy sum' . . . 'easy sum'. <u>Is that correct?</u> |
| **Chorus** | No. |
| **Teacher** | <u>Now, what is the correct answer?</u> Yahaya. |
| **Yahaya** | Today's sums is very easy. |
| **Teacher** | No, I just want you to choose a word from column B. Choose a word. <u>Is the word 'easy' correct?</u> |
| **Chorus** | Yes. |
| **Teacher** | Yes, the word easy is correct. 'Easy sum'. <u>Now, what do we say?</u> '<u>A easy sum</u>' or '<u>an easy sum</u>'? <u>Which is correct?</u> |
| **Chorus** | 'An easy sum'. |
| **Teacher** | Again. |
| **Chorus** | 'An easy sum'. |
| **Teacher** | We say 'an easy sum'. <u>You remember?</u> Easy—E—is a vowel. |

The second example involves one of the map tasks mentioned in Chapter 5. An adult elementary-level general English class are trying to mark a route according to recorded instructions. The speaker has just referred to 'the National Monument', which appears on their map as 'statue' (see Figure 6.1, page 111). They have agreed that they need to ask the teacher for more information.

*Example 6.2*

| | |
|---|---|
| **T** | ask me then |
| **I** | uh <u>where is the National Monument?</u> |
| **T** | on your map + it says 'statue' |
| **Ss** | <u>statue?</u> |
| **I** | *(points at his map)* <u>this one the National Monument?</u> |
| **O** | + + + <u>that's the National Monument?</u> |
| **T** | yes |
| **A** | + this your fault, O |
| **O** | <u>that's the National Monument?</u> |
| **I** | <u>did he say 'National Statue'?</u> |
| **T** | no the tape said 'National Monument' |
| **I** | yes |
| **T** | but on your map it says 'statue' + + it's the same thing |
| **I** | <u>the same name?</u> + <u>the same thing?</u> |
| **T** | yes + the statue is the National Monument |

M  <u>National?</u> + + <u>may you write?</u>
T  *(writes 'National Monument' on the board)*
O  + + statue is an ornament
I  yes
K  <u>what does statue mean?</u> + <u>is it a common word or something</u>
   <u>for plans?</u>
T  it's usually a figure of a person made from marble or stone
I  ah + figure
O  + + <u>statue of the John Knox you see?</u>
(observation data)

# Teacher–learner interaction

Those extracts come from rather different forms of speaking activity. In Example 6.1 there is some interaction between teacher and learners, but only in the sense that each speaking turn from the teacher is followed by one from an individual pupil or with a choral response. There is little communication; the questions the teacher asks require a response that she knows in advance. She asks them in order to confirm that the pupils know what she thinks they know. When a learner's response strays beyond the narrow limits of the desired answer ('Today's sums is very easy'), she refuses to accept it: 'No I just want you to choose a word from column B'.

This is unlike the sort of question and answer in Example 6.2. There the learners are really involved in negotiating meaning with the teacher and with each other. They also take the initiative in asking questions. The communication in Example 6.2 develops naturally within the context of the listening task.

Example 6.1 illustrates a familiar pattern of teacher–learner talk, which is a necessary part —but only a part—of classroom interaction: the cycle of Initiation–Response–Feedback.

| | | |
|---|---|---|
| **Teacher** | Is the word 'easy' correct? | *Initiation* |
| **Chorus** | Yes | *Response* |
| **Teacher** | Yes, the word 'easy' is correct | *Feedback* |

This routine can produce the *illusion* that a teacher is interacting with learners by asking questions and getting answers. But in the two cases in Example 6.1 where the teacher appears to encourage the pupils to give an individual response by using comprehension checks ('You understand, boys?' and 'You remember?'), it would probably require the courage of an Oliver Twist for a pupil to answer 'No, Miss'.

Patterns of interaction in classrooms vary from place to place, influenced by local educational norms, and also from time to time, as methodological fashions come and go. Example 6.1 was recorded in a West African primary school in the 1960s; Example 6.2 was recorded in Scotland nearly 30 years later. But time and place are not the only factors. The level and age of the class also makes a difference; the purpose of the current learning activity is another influence on interaction patterns.

Questioning patterns have been studied by a number of classroom researchers and have been shown to be a means by which teachers exert control over the interaction, and not simply a means of eliciting information. The term *display question* has been coined to refer to a question to which the teacher knows the answer in advance, as in the first of the two extracts. Questions that genuinely seek new information are called *referential* or *real* questions.

We should not assume that the 'display' questions in Example 6.1 simply reflect a bygone era or local traditions. In a study carried out in the early 1980s, Michael Long and Charlene Sato analysed teacher–learner interaction in elementary-level ESL classes in three states—Hawaii, California, and Pennsylvania—and found that on average only one in every seven questions asked by teachers was a 'real' question, i.e. one to which they did not know the answer (Long and Sato 1983). In general, most of the questions asked were for 'display', and feedback was limited to acceptance or rejection of learners' responses.

One reason for including 'real' questions is quantitative: learners tend to give longer responses than when we ask them 'display' questions (Brock 1984). Another is qualitative: if learners' classroom experience is one-sided, as passive responders to questions and instructions, they cannot practise taking the initiative in speaking. Thirdly, there is a risk that if teachers generally use questions to test students' knowledge, rather than to let them tell us what they have to say, that can discourage them from wanting to answer, even in that limited way. This point is well expressed by Manmatha Kundu, a teacher-trainer working in Orissa, India:

> Most of the time we talk in class hardly ever giving our students a chance to talk, except when we occasionally ask them questions. Even on such occasions, because we insist on answers in full sentences and penalize them for their mistakes, they are always on the defensive.
> (Kundu 1993: 13)

Even when teachers do decide to encourage real communication between students, it can be hard for us to move away from our traditional roles of controller and organizer. We can see this in Example 6.3, which comes from a general English lesson where lower-intermediate students are reporting the results of pair work to the rest of the class. Each pair has been asked to study two advertisement texts and to identify the criteria by which the products could be compared. Students M and V have been comparing adverts for cars, and now report back to the class.

*Example 6.3*

M   number one we talk about what kind of car + +
V   saloon + sport + +
M   yeah fastback + we also talk about 'displacement' + + *(looking at other students)* do you know 'displacement'?
T   I don't know
Ss  *(laugh)*
T   I wouldn't worry too much about that + + M is an expert *(writes on board)* 'an expert' + he knows a lot about cars + he knows a lot about the detail about it yes *(to J)* you are an economist I think?
J   yes
T   yes *(to class)* he's an expert in economics + or going to be + and an expert lawyer here + an expert syllabus designer + there + + yeah experts in your own fields + I am a *(writes on board)* 'non-expert' in a number of things + ok right + + so don't worry about 'displacement'
M   ok
T   carry on
(observation data)

This illustrates how teachers' intentions can conflict with their actions. The pairs have been working on different texts, in order to create a genuine information gap; nobody knows what is in the advertisements the others have analysed, nor what the outcome of that analysis is. When student

M uses the word 'displacement', he realizes that it may be unfamiliar to the others. In fact, he discovers that not even the teacher knows the word. This is an ideal platform for real negotiation of meaning, but instead of encouraging M to explain 'displacement', the teacher seems to see the situation as problematic. He takes over control of the interaction, telling M to go on to the next point, without 'worrying' about 'displacement'. As well as taking away from M the responsibility for explaining the word, the teacher imposes himself by initiating a teaching episode around the word 'expert', which *he* has used. An opportunity for real learner-led communication has been missed.

If we want to extend learners' competence in speaking, we have to know when to relax our control over classroom interaction, so as to give them the chance to practise freer talk. This does not mean that the classroom has to undergo total revolution or that teachers should abandon all control. But we should be including at least occasional activities which realign the communicative roles of teachers and learners, by enabling learners to take over responsibility for the interaction. The teacher still exercises control, but through choice of task, of grouping, and so on, and not by limiting the language the learners produce.

The British applied linguist Pit Corder once compared learning a foreign language with learning to play tennis (Corder 1981). When the 'speaking' that learners do is no more than a response to questions or instructions from the teacher, it does not take them beyond the basic practice of isolated strokes. But tennis coaches develop their pupils' skills by moving from single-stroke practice to playing each other in short games, giving them experience of using a variety of strokes in combination. In the same way, as well as setting up the necessary work on the basic speaking skills, teachers should be creating opportunities for interaction that allow freer language use.

# Learner–learner interaction

In Chapter 5 I suggested a number of ways of letting learners take the initiative in negotiating meaning *with the teacher* on listening tasks. But we also need to provide for negotiation of meaning *between learners*, through speaking tasks involving pairs or small groups. The idea of group work (including pair work) is not new, of course. The usual reasons given for using it are that simultaneous group work maximizes each learner's opportunity to speak and that practising in a small group reduces the psychological burden of public performance. To those arguments in favour of group work we can add the findings from classroom research:

- learners rarely pick up each other's errors, even in the short term (Porter 1986)
- learners express a wider range of language functions in group work (Long, Adams, McLean, and Castanos 1976)
- in group work on reading and listening comprehension, learners give fuller answers than in whole-class work with a teacher (Rulon and McCreary 1986)
- group work is more likely to lead to negotiation of meaning than inter-action with the teacher (Doughty and Pica 1986).

Although negotiation in group work has a number of advantages, some writers have expressed warnings about the need to introduce negotiation tasks with care. Guy Aston, working with EFL learners in Italy, doubted whether 'the more' negotiation necessarily meant 'the merrier' (Aston 1986). In particular, he saw a possible conflict between the teacher's purpose and the effect on learners. A task designed to raise communicative problems might well lead to the negotiation of meaning, but also to frustration on the learners' part. George Yule, writing from his experience of teaching graduate ESL classes in Louisiana, has recently made the point that what are supposed to be co-operative tasks can slip into confrontation and competition, with one partner trying to dominate the other (Yule 1994). This is what seems to be happening in Example 6.4, which comes from an interactive version of the map task featured in Example 6.2. Student L is being given instructions by student S for drawing a route; their two maps are slightly different (see Figure 6.1).

**Student L's version**          **Student S's version**

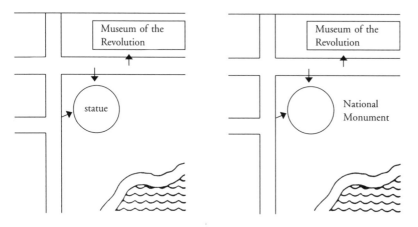

*Figure 6.1: Maps* (adapted from Brown 1986: 293)

At the point when we join them, S is about to refer for the first time to the National Monument:

**Example 6.4**

    S   We are using Palace Avenue.
    L   And then, uh, we meet the second cross.
    S   Cross and . . .
    L   There is the Statue there.
    S   You see, uh, the Mon-, Monument
    L   Monument?
    S   Just, eh, in front of you.
    L   Oh.
    S   In front of you.
    L   Oh, okay, yeah, yeah.
    S   Not turn, eh, up or down, okay?
    L   Okay, okay.
    S   That's it. Now . . .
    L   There's a monument, huh?
    S   Monument, monument.
    L   Okay.
    S   After that . . .
    L   Not a statue?
    S   Walk up, go, go down.
    L   Go down.
    S   Go down until the first cross.
    L   Go down until the first cross.
    S   First cross. After that . . .
(Luk 1994: 508)

When L tries to check the difference between S's authoritative map and his own, S's reply 'Monument, monument' suggests he is annoyed and losing patience. L says 'okay' but double-checks ('Not a statue?'). But S does not respond to the intended confirmation check; it may be that he does not hear what L says, or that he ignores it. The result is that L is left to make the best he can of the situation. He decides not to persist with further checking, possibly to avoid annoying S even more. Faced with S's insistence that the Monument is on the map, L resolves the difficulty by *adding* it to his map:

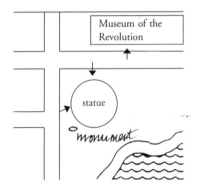

*Figure 6.2: Student L's solution*

In this way, L is able to reconcile the differences between his world and the speaker's. S's apparent annoyance with his listener is a reminder that classroom learning has affective and social dimensions. Learners are not neutral pawns in the teacher's game, but individuals with positive and negative feelings about themselves and others. One of the skills of teaching is knowing how to create a positive atmosphere. In the case of negotiation tasks, we have to persuade learners of the benefits on two levels: cognitive (that these tasks will help them learn) and affective (that they are enjoyable).

This means that it is important to create a co-operative atmosphere, in which feedback can be given without upsetting those who receive it. One way to set up the right expectations is to present and discuss examples of interaction between native and non-native speakers to demonstrate the value of repair and negotiation—as I have been doing in this book. This can help make learner–learner feedback seem a natural and necessary part of face-to-face communication, rather than as a personal attack on them by other students.

# Setting up negotiation tasks

## Introducing negotiation

One route towards learner–learner negotiation is through the sort of indirect negotiation tasks I described in Chapter 5, based on interaction with a text through the teacher. For students' first experience of fully interactive negotiation, I normally use a 'jigsaw speaking' activity. This is a form of ordering task, based on memory. You select or compose a text, cut it up into single sentences, and give one to every learner in a group for them to memorize. You then take back their sentences and they have to work out the original order of the text, without writing anything down. Once they have done that, they then dictate their sentences in the correct order, for everyone in the group to write out the original text. The text below is one I wrote for an elementary-level general English class, who had recently read about the ship *Queen Elizabeth II*.

> The *QE2* is the largest passenger ship in the world. She can carry about 2,000 people. They all have beautiful cabins to sleep in. The biggest is about ten metres by eight. It costs four times more than the smallest. There are many games and sports to play during the day. There are also dances and discos in the evenings. It must be very nice to travel on her.

As you will see, this simple text contains a number of linking words that the learners can use as clues as to the correct sequence. Different groups set about the task in different ways, but however they approach the problem, they can only solve it by everyone contributing their part of the puzzle. Example 6.5 shows one group of four students at the start of the first stage, where they are telling each other their sentences. H is from Spain, A and E are Japanese, and J comes from the Faroe Islands.

*Example 6.5*

E   yes + <u>the Queen + Queen Elizabeth</u>
H   Queen Elizabeth
E   <u>is the largest passenger + largest passenger</u>
J   the Queen is the largest passenger?
H   passenger?
E   <u>the Queen Elizabeth second</u>
A   hm?
E   sorry + I mistook + <u>Queen Elizabeth the second</u>
A   hmhm
H   it's the second?
E   <u>is the largest passenger in the</u>
H   in the?
E   <u>in the world</u>
A   yeah in the
H   in the?
J   in the boat?
E   <u>in the world</u>
H   in the bar?
E   <u>world</u>
H   in the?
E   world
J   in the w-o-r-l-d *(stretching the vowel)*
E   <u>in the world</u> yes
H   oh w-o-r-l-d
*(laughter)*
(observation data)

So even a 'simple' task such as saying a short sentence aloud from memory provides plenty of material for repair and negotiation. Yet, as I observed this group at work, student E showed no obvious signs of irritation at having his pronunciation of 'world' queried and then corrected by the others in the group. The laughter at the end suggests a relaxed and friendly atmosphere among the learners.

# Grouping

When setting up group work, one of the teacher's important decisions is who is to work with whom. In Chapter 1 I mentioned research by Evangeline Varonis and Susan Gass which suggested that the greater the differences between learners, the greater the natural need for negotiation. Of course our room for manœuvre may be limited; in most of the world's classrooms, learners come from a single background culture and share a common first language, so the teacher may not have the option of putting together speakers of different first languages when setting up communication tasks. Even so, the learners in any class are likely to vary in proficiency, and it should be possible to form groups of relatively 'unequal' partners. In a multilingual class it makes sense for people with different first languages *and* different levels to work together.

A higher-level learner may not want to work with a weaker partner. However, Patricia Porter has argued there are advantages for both partners in a mixed-level pair: the more proficient learner gets practice in producing comprehensible output; the weaker partner gains experience in negotiating meaning (Porter 1986).

But group work is not the only alternative to non-interactive whole-class work. In Chapter 4 I mentioned the Indian methodologist Karuna Kumar, who works in a context where large class size might be thought to make interaction and involvement difficult (Kumar 1992). His article shows that teachers can increase learners' opportunities to speak without resorting to group work. He describes how one teacher of a class of 45 pupils set up a play-reading, using a script from the class's textbook. Nearly half the class were directly involved in reading different parts, while the others listened in, prompted, commented on the readers' performances and gave the teacher ideas and suggestions. Kumar shows that by encouraging contributions from learners a teacher can create opportunities for learner talk in a large class, even without allowing what he calls the 'private talk' of groupwork. What matters, he says, is not class size, but attitudes; teachers should be prepared to include learners as 'co-participants in the activity and monitors of the classroom interaction' (Kumar 1992: 39).

# Distributing the information

A second important influence on learner–learner negotiation is whether each individual learner *has* to contribute for the task to succeed. The jigsaw speaking task I described earlier is an example of a *required information exchange task*: since each member of the group gets a sentence known only to them, the successful solution to the problem depends on everyone sharing that information with their partners. On the other hand, a discussion about smoking in public places is an *optional exchange task*: learners are free to contribute but may say little or even remain silent. From the point of view of interactive negotiation, the advantage of required information exchange tasks is that the distribution of the information between the learners guarantees the participation of all the members of the group. Since everyone's contribution also needs to be understood— again, unlike an open-ended discussion activity—there is a greater chance that the learners will negotiate meanings when necessary, bringing the benefits I discussed earlier.

Grouping and access to information can be interrelated. George Yule and colleagues at Louisiana State University have produced a series of studies on the effects of different combinations of learner pairing and informa- tion distribution (Yule 1990, 1991, 1994; Yule and Powers 1994; Yule, Powers, and Macdonald 1992). The negotiation tasks they studied were similar to the map tasks I have discussed in this book, where one partner (the sender) has an authoritative map showing a route and has to tell the other partner (the receiver) how to draw in the route on theirs. The researchers found that when the sender had higher proficiency than the receiver, they tended to impose an outcome—which was often inaccurate. Yule comments that 'The general effect was of a one-way performance by the higher proficiency sender' (Yule 1994: 196), as in the extreme case below.

*Example 6.6*
> S    it's not a turn
> R    it's REALLY A TURN
> S    no no no – okay it –
> R    if we call it a turn we can . . .
> S    okay okay if you – WILL YOU LISTEN TO ME PLEASE? okay listen to me – now
> (Yule 1994: 194)

S (the sender) appears to be acting alone, rather than interacting with R (the receiver); he is trying to dictate what R should have on his map. However, Yule and his colleagues found that when the lower-proficiency learner was in the sender role, a pair was more likely to negotiate collab- oratively and achieve a successful solution. That combination of level and access to information stands a better chance of leading to effective negoti- ation and so to a resolution of the communication puzzle. So who talks to whom (grouping) and who knows how much (distribution) are impor- tant factors to take into account in preparing a negotiation task.

# Feedback

We have seen that certain types of interaction task create opportunities for learners to negotiate meaning and to 'notice the gap'. Practice of this type is valuable, but we also need to give learners the feedback that can convert those opportunities into actual learning. (I am using the term 'feedback' to refer to any information about the success of the message.) In a talk to the 1982 TESOL Convention, Jacqueline Schachter compared the input necessary for language learning with the 'nutritional needs' of the human being (Schachter 1983). She described four basic forms of input to the learning process: negative or positive on one dimension, and implicit or explicit on the other (see Figure 6.3).

|  | *Implicit* | *Explicit* |
|---|---|---|
| *Positive* | clues showing the listener understands | confirmation (approval) |
| *Negative* | signals that repair is necessary | correction (disapproval) |

*Figure 6.3: Alternative forms of feedback*

## *Teacher–learner feedback*

As I mentioned in Chapter 1, it is rare in non-classroom conversation in English to find one speaker correcting the other explicitly; we prefer self-repair. This means that the teacher's role as corrector is relatively unusual, even if it is an accepted and even expected part of what we do in the class-room. As well as providing *cognitive* feedback (about the comprehensibil-ity or accuracy of what the learner has said), teachers give *affective* feedback (showing approval or disapproval). So there is a risk that, unless carefully handled, the act of correcting may impose an emotional burden on the learner.

As Figure 6.3 shows, correction is not the only form of negative feedback. Repair signals such as clarification requests are a more subtle indication that there are problems with what the speaker has said. One might assume that explicit feedback might be more effective than implicit, but there is some evidence that the opposite is true. Teresa Pica studied the way learn-ers working on pair tasks with a native speaker reacted to implicit neg-ative feedback from their partner (Pica 1988). She found that they made their output more comprehensible in 95 per cent of cases, and more ac-curate in almost half the cases. She also found that some native speakers tended to do the repair work for the learner (for example, by guessing at the intended form) and therefore relieved the learner of the responsibility for sorting out their problem. Under normal circumstances, this would be a helpful action, but perhaps in the classroom we should be less than completely co-operative, in order to push learners to greater accuracy. Although Pica's research was not a classroom study, it ties in with the findings of Studies 13 and 14 (in Chapter 4). Implicit negative feedback such as a request for clarification can be a more effective teaching device than explicit correction. By indicating a problem, but not immediately providing the solution, teachers may do more to facilitate learners' progress.

## *Learner–learner feedback*

More attention is now given to ways of encouraging feedback from learner to learner. Among the usual reasons for getting learners to take on the role of corrector and adviser are:

– it increases learners' speaking opportunities
– it develops a conscious focus on language form
– it encourages them to express their own judgements on language points
– it is an acknowledgement that different individuals know more about specific areas than others
– it provides an opportunity for real communication.

Learner-led group tasks can provide opportunities for peer feedback, but they bring potential risks, too. My experience is that some learners resent being corrected by other members of the group. This seems to apply particularly to the correction of pronunciation. Perhaps in this specific area of language performance the person being corrected feels that the pot is calling the kettle black; few learners of English have achieved such native-like pronunciation that their peers feel they have earned the right to correct others. Also there is no guarantee that learner–learner feedback will help the learner to notice the gap between what they have said and what they should have said. We can see this in Example 6.7, which comes from the same *QE2* jigsaw speaking task as Example 6.5.

*Example 6.7*

E    it must be very nice to travel on her *(sounds like 'ong ha')*
A    yes
H    it's?
E    it must be very nice
H    to travel
E    to travel ong ha
H    ong?

E    <u>ong ha</u>
H    ong ha?
E    <u>ong ha</u> + and next?
H    what's + what's mean 'ong ha'?
A    a ship + on a ship
H    a ship?
J    that's the ship + the boat + you know? + the Queen
A    ok
J    she is mentioned the Queen + vessels or ship they are + they always
H    ok ok
J    always she
(observation data)

E's faulty pronunciation of 'on her' is not explicitly corrected. Student H asks for clarification but gets only repetition from E. Finally student J explains that the word 'her/she' refers to ships, but he assumes that H has recognized 'ong ha' as 'on her'. So here negotiation has made E's speech more comprehensible but not more accurate—perhaps a case for teacher intervention, since peer feedback has been only partly successful here.

## Combining learner and teacher feedback

As Example 6.7 illustrates, it makes sense to provide feedback both from learners and from the teacher, since we cannot expect learners to spot all the points that require comment. The technique I like to use is in three steps and is based on an audio- or video-recording of the performance by the group you are going to comment on. The recording is replayed three times. On Replay 1, the class listen to—or watch—the performance a second time. But only the performers (the people in the recording) are allowed to stop the tape, in order to self-correct points which they notice when they have a second chance to monitor their speaking.

On Replay 2 the other learners can ask for the tape to be stopped, for them to suggest corrections or get confirmation from the teacher. But they have to find points other than those the performers have commented on during Replay 1.

Replay 3 is for me to draw attention to any further points not covered in the first two rounds of feedback.

The reason behind this three-step procedure is to do with the distinction between *slips* and *errors*, which I mentioned in Chapter 4. Replay 1 gives the performers a chance to 'edit' their speaking in the way you might edit a piece of your own writing, picking up slips that you are able to correct yourself as you re-read what you have written. Replay 2 allows the observers to comment on points that the performers have not noticed;

these might be either slips or errors. If the class is of mixed nationality, then it is more likely that the observers will spot errors; if all the class are from the same language background, they may share the same errors and not notice them in other learners' speech.

Replay 3 is the opportunity for the teacher to highlight gaps that none of the class have noticed. For example, in the lesson where the group of four students were recorded doing the QE2 task, I played them Examples 6.5 and 6.7, to focus attention on the Japanese student E's pronunciation of the /ɜ/ vowel in 'world' and 'her' as /ɑ/. He was aware that something was causing his listeners a problem, but he had not realized exactly what it was. I used the recording to show that how the implicit feedback from our listeners (in this case, 'boat?' and 'bar?' for 'world', 'ha?' for 'her') can tell us what our speech sounds like to other people. I asked the other students to suggest word pairs that E could practise saying to make the difference clearer (e.g. 'fast/first', 'bath/birth').

I have focused here on pronunciation, but of course that is only one of the aspects of language use that may deserve comment at the feedback stage. We should try to make feedback relevant to the specific task, as well as to the general needs of the students. For example, at the first stage of jigsaw speaking, when they are trying to make the precise content of their sentences clear, pronunciation is particularly important. For other types of speaking activity, such as role play, we need to broaden the feedback. Table 6.1 sets out four aspects of speaking and also makes clear the order of priority for the task, by placing 'language' after the other three.

| Strategy | Did they manage to get what they wanted? Did one player come off the loser? |
|---|---|
| Information | Did they use relevant role information provided? Did they forget or change any details? |
| Communication | Were there any breakdowns in communication? How (and how well) did they resolve them? |
| Language | Did they appear to manage to express their intended meaning? Did their performance reveal any significant gaps in grammar, vocabulary, or pronunciation? |

*Table 6.1: Sample feedback sheet* (from Lynch and Anderson 1992: 94)

Although it probably takes more effort to give learners feedback on 'strategy', 'information', and 'communication' than on language points, it helps to draw their attention to more important aspects of speaking, such as the ability to negotiate meaning. It also reminds the teacher to think about overall success on a task and not just about how correct the language was.

No single feedback technique has yet been shown to be the key to more effective learning. Even those techniques that have produced positive results in the form of learning may have done so only in the short term. On the other hand, we cannot assume that if no learning effect is immediately obvious, no learning is taking place. Some learners simply take longer to learn the new item. Since speaking is so complex and learning is hard to measure, a reasonable conclusion is that we should use a variety of types of feedback in the classroom.

# Summary

In this chapter I have discussed how the traditional patterns of classroom interaction affect the speaking roles that learners are allowed to adopt. By including interaction tasks in which learners can take the communicative initiative, we can provide them with a wider and richer experience of speaking. Of particular importance are tasks leading to the negotiation of meaning, since they practise the strategies learners will need for sorting out problems in real-life communication. In addition to the practical experience of making themselves understood, learners benefit from the opportunity to analyse and get feedback on their performances on interactive tasks, to discuss negotiation episodes, and to compare notes on specific examples of what went well (and what did not). Above all, experience of negotiation episodes gives learners a realistic view of what to expect in real-life encounters with the language they are learning.

## *Suggestions for further reading*

*Teaching speaking skills*
**Bygate, M.** 1987. *Speaking.* Oxford: Oxford University Press. This book examines different approaches to the teaching of speaking and illustrates them with samples from a wide range of published materials.

*Negotiation and repair*
**Aston, G.** 1986. 'Trouble-shooting in interaction: the more the merrier?' *Applied Linguistics* 7/2: 128–43. An article about some of the problems of using tasks that are intended to lead to negotiation of meaning.

*Learner–learner interaction*
**Porter, P.** 1986. 'How learners talk to each other: input and interaction in task-centered discussions.' in R. Day (ed.): *Talking to Learn: Conversation in Second Language Acquisition.* Rowley, Mass.: Newbury

House. A clearly written research paper that summarizes the advantages of group work and, in particular, of grouping higher- and lower-level learners together.

### Communicative effectiveness

**Yule, G.** and **M. Powers.** 1994. 'Investigating the communicative outcomes of task-based interaction.' *System* 22/1: 81–91. Yule and Powers discuss a system by which teachers can evaluate the success of learners' performances in information-gap tasks.

### Feedback techniques

**Nolasco, R.** and **L. Arthur.** 1987. *Conversation.* Oxford: Oxford University Press. A practical book with plenty of ideas for speaking tasks; it contains a particularly good section on feedback.

# 7  TEACHING READING

In this chapter I apply ideas on the comprehension process (from Chapter 2) and on interactive comprehension strategies (from Chapter 5) to the design of classroom reading tasks. My suggestions relate to the selection of reading material and to ways of helping learners to interact with texts and with each other as they discuss material they have read or are in the process of reading.

## *Activity*

### A difficult text

The book review below is difficult in a number of ways. As you read it, monitor any problems you encounter and see how you deal with them. When you have finished, think about these questions:

1 Would you consider using the text with learners of English?
2 If so, with what level or type of learner would you use it?
3 Would you modify it in any way?

*Example 7.1*

**Lucy Tuck**

To begin with, I found Jonathan Coe's **What a Carve Up!** (Viking £10.99) too embarrassingly obvious: the flat blokeish prose, groaning under its freight of passé po-mo self-co; the easy-PC targets (arms trade, agribusiness, journalism). But I was wrong. Ghastlier than *Mary Shelley's Frankenstein*, longer than *The Fermata*, and a *$@!*£ sight more @&*%!*$ than *How Late It Was, How Late*, this novel has tremendous biro. I also enjoyed E Annie Proulx's gusty **The Shipping News** (Fourth Estate £5.99), and the seductive certainties of **German Printmaking in the Age of Goethe** by Antony Griffiths and Frances Carey (British Museum Press £19.95).

(The *Observer*, 20 November 1994)

As it stands, this review seems to be suitable only for very advanced learners of English, perhaps specializing in English literature, who might benefit from explanation of the literary allusions and the word play in the text. However, I have used the text with intermediate-level non-specialists, for a rather different purpose and without any modification, as I explain later in this chapter.

# Choice of texts: authenticity

Decisions about which texts to use with a specific group of learners raise the question of authenticity. The definition that most teachers accept is that authentic texts are samples of language used by and for native speakers. This suggests that texts are either authentic or inauthentic. It is true that in some cases it is easy to distinguish between language that is 'real' and language that is not; for instance, the dialogue between Klaus and the West family (Example 5.1) is obviously not a transcript of spontaneous talk.

But authenticity is not a black-or-white issue. It is difficult to accept the common definition of authentic as 'produced by native speakers for native speakers', because it would mean, for example, that a BBC World Service news bulletin would have to be regarded as inauthentic, since the intended audience is made up predominantly of non-native listeners. It also raises the question of what we mean by a native speaker—a fully competent adult user of the language? If so, what about the two 'Oscar ceremony' items (Examples 2.6 and 2.7)? Is the second inauthentic (or possibly less authentic) because it was intended for a child audience?

To resolve the problem of defining authenticity, Henry Widdowson suggested separating two aspects of communication: 'genuineness' and 'authenticity' (Widdowson 1979). He said that a text is genuine if it conforms to the conventions of that type of text—grammatical, lexical, etc.—whether or not it is an actual text, i.e. a text that has been used for some purpose other than teaching the language. So if a teacher composes a letter to use in class, it will be as good as an actual letter, provided it looks and sounds like one. Authentic, in Widdowson's view, should be used to describe an appropriate response of reader or listener to the text. Take the weather forecast item in Chapter 5 (page 95). This is genuine but invented. One possible authentic listener response to it would be for learners to take a decision about where to go that day; an inauthentic response might involve them listening for all the words ending with *-ly*.

If we accept that division, then we can think of authenticity as the *end* of language teaching. Whether or not the *means*, the text, is invented or discovered, does not matter. We should not be over-concerned with finding real texts; realistic texts will do just as well, provided they are used in a way that helps learners to respond to them appropriately.

# Interaction with texts

In this section I am using *interaction* in the sense of 'interactive processing', described in Chapter 2. There I commented on the interplay between three main comprehension resources: background knowledge, context, and knowledge of the language. As you read the Lucy Tuck review at the beginning of this chapter, you probably found yourself using those sources in trying to understand the problematic parts of the text.

For most learners, reading a text seems more straightforward than listening to one, for a number of reasons. Firstly, the actual process of reading makes it easier to monitor our comprehension; when listening we have little or no control over the speed at which the message is delivered, or the order in which we hear the different elements of the message. Secondly, the written (or printed) text presents the information in a more helpful way than is usually possible in speech. It is presented as clear letters, rather than in the relatively degraded sounds of natural speech; it is permanently fixed on the page, rather than as fleeting spoken utterances; and it is conveniently separated into words with blank spaces between them, rather than in a continuous stream.

These differences mean that the reader has quicker and easier access to more textual information than is available in the equivalent spoken version of the same message. Even so, particular texts are hard to make sense of; in Example 7.1 you may have found it hard to understand the author's use of the string of characters, '@&*%!*$!', which were used for particular effect. We will shortly see what sense a group of learners of English made of them.

## *Think-aloud interpretation*

One way to bring learners' interactive processing out into the open is to get them to explain their current interpretation of a text. This is an adaptation of a research technique known as a 'think-aloud procedure', used to investigate individual readers' routes to comprehension. The principle is similar to that of the paused listening task (Chapter 5). However, the difference is that in a think-aloud reading task each learner has the text in front of them and is also free to search the text for comprehension clues. In a paused listening task the stopping of the tape forces the learners to rely on their memory of what they have heard. So the two types of classroom task each reflect the differences in the real-life processes of reading or listening.

But why compare learners' interpretations? You could argue that every person's comprehension processes are bound to be individual, so there is little to be gained from discussing them. But my experience is that think-aloud tasks make some learners aware of textual clues which other learners in the group have recognized, which would pass unnoticed in individual reading.

Example 7.2 is an extract from a recording of a group of six post-intermediate learners of English. They have just been given the book review from the opening Activity on page 123.

*Example 7.2*

T    what I'm interested in is this part under <u>Lucy Tuck</u>
Ss   *(read for about 10 seconds)*
F    it doesn't look like English *(laughs)*
Ss   *(some laughter)*
T    no well bits of it aren't *(laughs)* so can you tell me + + in general terms first of all what + + sort of text is it
F    about books + + a critic of books + + how do you call the people who analyse the books?
T    the people + you're right + they are called critics + what is it they + write though? + + + *(to student O)* what did you spend time on in our September class?
O    criticism + + ah + critical review
T    ok + how did you know it was a critical review?
F    because he is giving his opinion about a book
T    but how do you know it was about a book?
F    + + + it has a review style *(laughs)*
Ss   *(laugh)*
T    all right + can you give me any other information about how you know it's a review
K    <u>Viking</u>
T    yes?
K    I don't know exactly but I think it's the publisher
T    ok any + other + + clues you used?
F    <u>novel</u>
K    /ʤɔ:'nætæn kɔ:z/
F    novel yes + sorry K you said?
K    /ʤɔ:n/ + + just before the title
T    oh right + <u>Jonathan Coe's</u> + right + ah how do you know + that's the title?
O    <u>bold</u>
T    it's in bold yes + did everybody read this bit here *(the page heading)* <u>Christmas Books</u> at the top?
M    no

T   oh + so + how soon + when you read the text how soon + in the text did you know it was about a book + can you remember?

M  when I read <u>this novel</u>

T   where's that + + ok two thirds of the way down + + so did Lucy Tuck like *What a Carve Up?* + or not

F   no she didn't

T   because?

F   <u>too obvious</u>

T   hmhm + *(to others)* do you agree? did Lucy Tuck like the book?

H  she did enjoy it + + because she says <u>I also enjoyed</u>

T   and?

H  <u>also</u> makes me know she + liked the *What a Carve Up*

T   so + + what about <u>too obvious</u> + + first of all does everybody agree that <u>too obvious</u> is negative?

Ss  yes

H  is always negative + in English but not in my language

T   so isn't that + + a problem then? + H says she enjoyed it but F says <u>too obvious</u>

H  but it was wrong

T   how do you know?

H  she wrote <u>I was wrong</u>

T   does she give any other indication in the text that + she did like the book? + apart from <u>I was wrong</u> + + + near the beginning + + + let me help a bit + + how did you understand <u>to begin with</u> in the first line?

F   at the beginning I think it was not a good book + + now I suppose it's good

T   and how did you understand <u>to begin with</u> before?

F   I understood just + simply as 'the first thing I want to say'

T   exactly + + so <u>to begin with</u> can mean 'firstly' + + then a list of reasons for example + or it can mean 'at first' + in a time + + time sequence +

(observation data)

My reason for choosing to use this text with this group was the difficulty I had myself with a number of words, such as 'po-mo' and 'biro'. I assumed this was because I am not familiar with the vocabulary of literary criticism. Nevertheless, I was able to work out roughly what the words meant. I decided to use the text with the students in Example 7.2, not to teach specific vocabulary, but to encourage a general attitude: I wanted them to realize that native readers, too, have problems with some texts, so that they might feel more relaxed about coping with their difficulties in understanding the foreign language.

When I used the text in class, I found that the group's discussion did seem to lead to learning—at least to the students' noticing features of English in the short term. At the end of their discussion, which continued for a further five minutes or so after the end of Example 7.2, I told them about my own problems in interpreting bits of the text such as 'biro' (which turns out to have been a misprint for 'brio') and asked them to think for 30 seconds or so and then to make a written note of something they felt they had learnt from the reading or from the think-aloud discussion. Below are the notes written by the six learners:

1 'review' = crítica *(translation into Spanish)*
2 Remember: look at headings!
3 Even our English teachers can have problems
4 Always, the word <u>too</u> is negative
5 Viking is a publisher
6 I have learnt one expression to take care about: 'to begin with' has Time meaning or List meaning

At the end of Chapter 2 I referred to Assia Slimani's finding that what different learners pick up in a lesson varies enormously from person to person. These six learners' notes on the Lucy Tuck review show exactly that variation in what these learners noticed: points about English (notes 1, 4, and 6), about real-world knowledge (note 5), and about the process of reading (notes 2 and 3). As you can see, the learner who wrote note 3 seems to have picked up for himself (since I had not told them what the teaching point was) what I had in mind when I decided to use this particular text and task.

Note 2 is also interesting, because it was written by the student who only realized the text was about books when she encountered the word 'novel'. The 'gap' she had noticed was the difference between the other learners' use of title information and her own strategy of reading line by line.

## Reciprocal teaching

Sara Cotterall of Victoria University in New Zealand has devised a more formalized version of the think-aloud task, based on a technique developed for remedial mother tongue teaching, called 'reciprocal teaching' (Cotterall 1990). This involves learners working in groups and taking turns as instructor or leader, guiding the other members of the group through their reading of a text.

The groups work through a text one paragraph at a time. For each paragraph a different person is chosen to lead them through four discussion stages: clarifying any problems encountered in the text, stating the main idea, summarizing the content of the paragraph, and predicting the likely content of the next paragraph. At each stage the other learners offer feed-back on the leader's comments, as shown in Example 7.3, where learner S2 is acting as instructor:

*Example 7.3*

    S1 What does it mean "procedure"?
    S2 "Procedure" Ah—"procedure" means . . .
    S3 A step or ah further –
    S2 "Procedure" means ah –
    S3 Proceed?
    S2 No.
    S4 Step in –
    S3 Step.
    S2 All the steps together in one.
    S1 Procedure.
    S2 Do you understand? Procedure is is ah is ah you do something and ah from the start to the beginning, and from the start to the beginning that what you do is a procedure. I think. Anything else?
    S1 One more – "X-ray"?
    S2 X-ray is ah when you go to hospital – with a broken leg and then *(laughter)*
    S1 Ahah.
    S2 X-ray. You know?
    S1 Yes.
    S2 Anything else?
    S1 No.
    (Cotterall 1990: 60–1)

As the discussion on a paragraph is completed, the leader nominates another student to take over. The teacher's role is to act as discussion leader at least once each session (to provide a model for the learners to follow), to monitor the interaction, and to intervene when the peer instruc-tion reaches a dead end or takes a wrong turning.

Cotterall argues that the value of the reciprocal teaching technique is that it involves active problem-solving, makes learners more conscious of their reading style, and also requires the sort of negotiation of meaning that is thought to generate language learning.

## Modifying a text

My third example of an activity highlighting the interaction between reader and text is one I have adapted from a task described by Guy Cook of the University of Leeds (Cook 1989). The learners are given the passage below and are asked to think about how they would shorten the text to meet the needs of a specific group of readers: a child, the mayor of Oak Park (mentioned in the text), and a Martian anthropologist, among others.

> Ernest Hemingway was born indoors in 1899 at Oak Park, a highly respectable suburb of Chicago, a large city in the USA, where his father, a keen sportsman, was a doctor. He was the second of six children. For short periods each year, the family spent holidays in a lakeside hunting lodge in Michigan, near Indian settlements. They spent the time there swimming and walking, and when the holidays were over they used to return home. The young Ernest, who grew older as the years passed by, attended a local school, and although energetic and successful in all school activities, he twice ran away from home, though he returned on both occasions. When he left school, he joined the *Kansas City Star* as a cub reporter in 1917. At that time there was a war raging in Europe, and the next year he volunteered as an ambulance driver on the Italian front and was badly wounded during an attack by the enemy army. This prevented him from continuing his work. Returning to America he began to write features for a newspaper called the *Toronto Star Weekly* in 1919, and in 1921 was married of his own free will to a woman he had met and fallen in love with earlier. That year he came to Europe by boat as a roving correspondent and covered several large conferences. He ate food every day and slept at night.
> (Cook 1989: 92)

As you will have realized, Cook's text contains redundant information of various types: some would be taken for granted by any reader, such as the fact that Hemingway grew older as the years passed by; and some would be known to some readers, for example that there was a war in Europe in 1917.

The task requires the learners to think about the relationship between a reader's background knowledge and the information the writer needs to include in the text. As they discuss what they can expect a particular group of readers to know, the learners are also made to think about the information they themselves needed as they were reading the passage.

I have now used this text with a variety of classes, including lower-intermediate students of general English, advanced-level students of English for academic purposes, and native and non-native teachers of English. It is always a great success; apart from being entertaining, it produces lots of points for discussion, and I have been impressed by the quality of the learners' arguments over whether or not certain items of information are necessary. I have used it with both general English and academic English students, and each lesson has produced some new insight on the information in the text. For example, a Dutch medical student managed to persuade her group that the phrase 'during an attack by the enemy army' should *not* be deleted. Her argument was that since 40 per cent of United States casualties in the Vietnam war were caused by so-called 'friendly fire', we should not assume that Hemingway had not been shot by his own side.

To give a flavour of the discussion that Cook's task leads to, here is a short extract (Example 7.4) showing a group of six students at work on the text. I had asked the students—from Korea, Spain, Brazil, Mozambique and Taiwan—to discuss possible modifications to the text for one of three audiences: (1) 14-year-old children from the United States, (2) Canadian adults, (3) undergraduate students of English literature from their own country. This group chose to discuss the needs of the under-graduates.

**Example 7.4**

    **F**  leave out <u>He was the second of six children</u> + I think
    **V**  why?
    **F**  this is not necessary
    **V**  no?
    **B**  yes it's not + + related to the reader + not relevant + + to the reader
    **H**  no it is important I think + + and relevant so + we keep it
    **B**  why? + + it doesn't matter how big is his family
    **H**  yes it is very necessary + + our readers study English books
    **M**  literature literature
    **H**  yes so + Hemingway is writer + + so + +
    **M**  childhood is important time for writers
    **B**  it's important for everybody I think + + isn't it true?
    **M**  yes but influence specially for writers
    **L**  the old brother oldest brother is always powerful + and if Hemingway was oldest he had more + + strong powerful personality
    **H**  so his writing would also be strong maybe + that is our opinion
    **B**  but + + I am the oldest brother + in my family + + so do you think I am very strong and + powerful?
    **L**  not in English writing but + in your language yes
    **Ss**  *(laugh)*
(observation data)

That extract shows how learners doing this sort of task have to take their readers into account and then to justify decisions about changes to the text, as they prepare to persuade students from another group that those decisions are reasonable. This way of getting learners to adapt texts for different audiences actively engages their awareness of language and content. As such, it can be seen as part of the general movement in language teaching away from a primary concern with linguistic correctness towards a balanced view of communication, which also emphasizes the role of background knowledge as part of the message.

# Interaction about texts

In the previous section I focused on interaction in the psychological sense, the use of a variety of clues in making sense of a text. Of course the classroom is not simply a setting for this sort of internal individual process; it is also an arena for social interaction. In this section I would like to concentrate specifically on the interaction *between* students working on a reading text. For many generations of language learners, 'reading' has meant doing comprehension questions, and most of us take it for granted that, at some point in the process of reading a text, the learners should be asked to answer questions about it. Questions enable us to check what they have understood and can also help the learners to read better:

> The questions that help you to understand are the ones that make you work at the text. They force you to contribute actively to the process of making sense of it, rather than expecting understanding just to happen.
> (Nuttall 1982: 125)

Of course, a great deal depends on what sort of questions we ask and which aspects of a text we draw learners' attention to. Answers may involve retrieving explicitly stated facts, inferring implied meanings, expressing opinions on content, among other things. But in general, the model of classroom interaction assumed in the asking of comprehension questions is the traditional three-phase model presented in Chapter 6: the teacher asks a comprehension question, probably taken from exercises following the reading text; a student gives an answer; and the teacher accepts or rejects it.

If we want to encourage learner–learner interaction about reading texts, we need to explore other possibilities. One is simply to use group work, so that learners compare and discuss their individual answers to the comprehension questions set by the course writer. This certainly increases the quantity of speaking practice, but it could also be seen as simply delaying the point at which the teacher confirms the Correct Answer after the groups have worked through the questions. I do not doubt the value of questions, but the problem I see in teaching reading interactively is how to develop a learner-centred approach to questioning the text.

# Question-setting

One radical proposal for using reading texts in the classroom has come from Sidney Whitaker of the University of North Wales: that it should be learners rather than teachers who think up and ask the questions (Whitaker 1983). Whitaker based his proposal on the general observation that in daily life we learn by 'interrogating the environment', searching for clues to confirm our understanding of novel events. Inside the classroom, on the other hand, things are conventionally rather different. There the teacher knows all the answers, so the learners' task is basically to read the teacher's mind. The fact that teachers are, in Whitaker's words, 'tuned into' particular answers can close our minds to other interpretations—such as the Dutch student's view of friendly fire in the Hemingway text.

Whitaker argued that if we allow learners to ask each other about the text, the questions they ask will be relevant to their own developing understanding of a text, to *their* current perceptions of what is important and difficult in the text. I have found that, given the chance to set their own questions, some learners ask each other *display* questions to which they have an answer, while others ask *real* questions about points they have not understood. Either way, the questions they ask match their current understanding of the text, which will change and develop as they read further.

Some teachers may be uncomfortable with the suggestion that we should relax our control over questions (and answers), so I would like to show how Whitaker's proposal works out in practice. Example 7.5 shows the progress of a discussion in which a class of my intermediate-level students worked in small groups on a number of short reading texts containing ambiguous information. Each group read a different text, discussed their interpretations, and then composed the questions they wanted another group to answer.

In their task instructions, I told them that their questions did not need to be ones they knew the answer to themselves, and that there could be a single correct answer or a number of possible answers. When they had completed their discussion and agreed on their questions, they passed the text and their questions to another group for them to read and answer. Here is the text that one group worked on:

> When I first went into the System, I had to queue for ages. At first the woman did not understand what I asked for, but eventually she found the bottles I wanted. Just as I was about to pay, the red light went on. It was a good thing that I had my passport with me.

In the extract below, one trio of students (L, J, and H) are answering the questions devised by three others (M, N, and K). I asked student L to read out the questions they were given, and then their answers, for the question-setters to confirm or reject.

**Example 7.5**

T   your first question was?
L   'Where was it?'
H   at the System
M   at the . . .?
H   at the System
M   I don't understand that
H   because S is capital one
    *(laughter)*
M   no I mean I don't understand System
J   but we answered your question
    *(laughter)*
T   your question was 'Where was it?' + their answer is 'at the System'
    + + next question?
L   next question + 'What does System mean?'
J   it means name of shop
M   a name of shop
T   the name of a shop
J   the name of a shop
M   ok
T   you accept that?
M   uhuh
T   good + third question?
L   'What is the woman's job?'
J   answer + shop assistant
T   that's agreed?
Ss  *(nod)*
T   fourth one?
L   'What was she/he doing?'
T   *(to M)* this is the narrator of the text you mean?
M   hmhm
T   so what's the answer?
L   he was buying bottles
    *(laughter)*
M   yes + buying drinks + bottles of drink
H   how do you know it's drink?
M   well + because we imagined a situation + a free shop in an airport
T   but there are bottles in the duty-free shop that you don't drink
M   yeah but we deal with statistics
    *(laughter)*

T  oh I see *(laughs)* you mean the probability is . . .

M  yeah when I don't know something I use the statistics

T  fine + the next question?

L  'What was the red light?'

J  no idea

H  signal

J  oh yeah some + kind of signal

M  yes but what kind of signal?

T  ah that's another question *(laughter)* + + I'm afraid they're only answering your written questions + + and the last one?

L  'Why was it a good thing?'

T  and your answer?

J  because he could identify himself with it

L  with passport

M  he could identify himself?

L  using his passport

H  at airport

T  no?

M  it don't make sense for me

K  for me I agree

T  oh sorry + do you mean that their answer doesn't match your answer + or + + their answer doesn't make sense but you don't have an answer either?

M  hmhm

   *(laughter)*

T  in other words is this a test question or a real question?

M  both

   *(laughter)*

M  my answer is different + I must explain I think it's a duty free shop in an airport + trying to buy something

T  yes

M  he has to wait for a long time + but when he + + saw the red light he saw he had to + + show the shoppings to somebody + so he gave up + to shop

T  oh he + had to show + what he had bought?

M  yeah the customs

T  but why the passport?

H  I think it was time to get airplane + I think it was almost time

T  is that possible do you think? + + the red light stopped him shopping because he had to catch his plane?

M  I don't think so + have you ever see a red light to tell you to get the plane? + + + I know just green light and red light for customs

J  I think duty free shop is inside customs so he didn't have to show the passport inside

> N no in my country we have to show passport to buy
> J no boarding card
> N oh I see yeah
> H we don't show boarding card and we don't show passport
> T so how do they know you're a passenger?
> K they don't give goods directly to me + + but they just send it directly to + the plane
> T really?
> K yes + so I can get the goods
> T + + sorry? + you can or you can't?
> K I can + + + I can get + + it's possible for me . . .
> *(laughter)*
> K . . . to get the goods on the plane
> N but then I need something to buy duty free in the customs + I need something
> J what?
> N maybe boarding pass + or passport
> H in my country the shops are inside the waiting room
> N hmhm ok
> H so we don't need to show anything
> (observation data)

That extract shows how learners' discussion of text content can naturally spread beyond the linguistic details of the text. The social interaction mirrors psychological interaction; they make connections with personal experiences, previous texts, factual background knowledge, cultural assumptions, and so on.

Example 7.5 also shows the teacher in the role of prompter and conductor, even though it is the learners who ask each other the questions. In other situations the learners may want the teacher to provide extra background information, as we can see in Example 7.6, which comes from the same discussion of the *Observer* book review as Example 7.2. Here the learner–learner interaction has reached an impasse, which can be resolved only by further information. The students are discussing the two odd strings of characters in the text.

### Example 7.6
> F why the strange keys + symbols?
> K to put words that is not allowed to say + + or write
> F ah + + bad words?
> K I think + yes + rude words
> F ah ok
> M you mean like + + censorship?
> F I think but I don't know

M  but do you know or + do you think + in the *Observer* was a censorship?

F  perhaps

M  but the *Observer* is not a conservative paper I think + I don't know but I think

K  we can ask the teacher + + is the *Observer* a conservative newspaper?

T  no not + + conservative by British standards

M  oh + so maybe . . .

(observation data)

Here we have a case where learners ask their own questions and for the most part contribute their own answers; they try out plausible solutions to the problems they have identified in the text—in this case, the reason for the reviewer's use of the string of symbols. But notice how they make use of the teacher: he is not asked to supply the correct answer to the main question (about the symbols), but to give them socio-cultural information (about the political stance of the *Observer*), which might help them to solve the problem for themselves. They refer to the teacher, rather than defer to him. He is called in when they need him and in a role that they define.

It might, in fact, be more appropriate to call this section 'Interaction *around* texts', rather than *about* texts, to emphasize that the text becomes a platform for negotiation of content, i.e. what the writer meant. In the negotiation process some learners may bring in background information that others do not have, which leads in a natural way to peer-teaching of new facts about culture, geography, science, etc.

All this is very different from the traditional procedure, where learners are given 8 or 10 questions, for each of which the materials writer (or teacher) has probably decided on a single answer. (Incidentally, we should not forget that those answers have been worked out after repeated readings of the text, by someone who is a fluent reader and competent user of the language). By getting learners to ask their own questions, teachers can direct attention to the *process* of understanding the foreign language. Traditional question procedures focus on the *product* of comprehension.

# Summary

In this chapter I have discussed ways of setting up reading activities that raise learners' awareness of their different individual interactions with reading texts. We have seen how work on reading texts—particularly, unmodified and difficult texts—can lead to the negotiation of meaning (the means) and negotiation of content (the end).

I have highlighted the role of such interaction as part of classroom learning, and shown how what is on the surface a 'reading task' can provide for integrated use of the foreign language among the learners, requiring the use of listening and speaking skills in the process of interaction. This type of interactive task is a valuable complement to more traditional classroom tasks. Whenever we can, we should bring in an interactive dimension—both with and about texts—to extend the learners' experience of the language.

## Suggestions for further reading

### Teaching reading

**Nuttall, C.** 1982. *Teaching Reading Skills in a Foreign Language*. London: Heinemann. A clear and comprehensive book on the practicalities of teaching reading.

**Wallace, C.** 1992. *Reading*. Oxford: Oxford University Press. Brings Nuttall's book up to date, in some ways. This book deals particularly well with the social side of reading.

**West, M.** 1955. *Learning to Read a Foreign Language*. London: Longman. A pioneering collection of papers, some written as early as the 1920s. Ahead of its time and still very relevant.

### Reading processes

**Carrell, P., J. Devine,** and **D. Eskey** (eds.). 1988. *Interactive Approaches to Second Language Reading*. Cambridge: Cambridge University Press. This collection of papers includes both theoretical and practical articles. ('Interactive' in its title is used in the sense of 'interactive processing' in my Chapter 2.)

### Authenticity

**Widdowson, H. G.** 1979. *Explorations in Applied Linguistics*. Oxford: Oxford University Press. Chapter 12 is a very helpful discussion of the complexities of authenticity.

# 8 TEACHING WRITING

In this chapter I discuss what happens in the process of writing, how teachers can create an interactive framework for writing, and how readers can respond to learners' written texts in ways which will make their writing better and clearer. This will involve looking at three participant roles in classroom writing: the writer, the reader, and the teacher.

## Writing as interaction

The heading of this section may strike you as odd. After all, *interaction* usually refers to spoken communication where there are literally 'actions between' people, either face to face or perhaps on the telephone. When writing, on the other hand, we usually have no audience present to react to our message as it is being formulated; the readers wait somewhere in the future. Indeed, the lack of an immediate audience is one reason why writing is sometimes more demanding than speaking:

> Writing as an activity that I am indulging in at the moment is not simply composing. What I am doing (successfully or not) is developing a discussion and arranging points in such a way as to persuade you, the reader, that I have something worthwhile to say. What is involved in this activity? There is certainly more to it than simply putting sentences together in sequence like wagons in a train. A good deal of time is spent going over what has previously been written and pondering how the discourse might most effectively develop from it. Thus, what I am writing now is dependent on my recollection of what has gone before. It is also dependent on how I think what I have written so far will be understood and on what I assume to be common ground between myself, the writer and you, the reader.
> (Widdowson 1978: 62)

So the writer has to take on the roles of both speaker and listener, who in spoken interaction would share responsibility for negotiating meaning. An effective writer is one who manages to anticipate what the imagined reader wants or needs to know, and at which point in the message they need to know it.

## *Decomposition*

One way of taking learners 'behind the scenes' of the production of a piece of writing is to use the technique of *decomposition* (Widdowson 1979: 177), which requires learners to reorganize a written text into the separate speaking turns of the dialogue that underlies it. Let me decompose for you a letter I received recently. Although letters are perhaps the type of writing that is most similar to spoken interaction—particularly if they are written for one specific individual—they also illustrate the basic interactive characteristics of writing in general.

The background to the letter is as follows. In January 1994 I sent a batch of slide films to be developed at the Filmex laboratory, but one of the films was not returned to me. There was then an exchange of letters with the laboratory, followed by silence for six months. In October 1994 I received the letter shown below.

*Example 8.1*

```
Dear Dr Lynch,

In response to your correspondence
concerning missing photographic material.
As you may already be aware, we currently
receive up to 50 films per week without
either return address or where the return
address has become separated during transit
to our Laboratory. We have thoroughly
examined all of these unclaimed films but
have not been able to match any with your
enquiry.

On Monday 28 November through to Thursday
1 December 1994, we will be holding a
series of open evenings so that all
customers can have a look for themselves
at all these outstanding films to try and
locate their missing material. We would
ask you to arrive at 6.00 p.m.—7.00 p.m.,
have a tour of our processing laboratory
and then look through the outstanding
films. Light refreshments will be available
along with the opportunity to discuss any
```

product queries with staff from the Filmex
Technical Department. If you would like to
attend one of these open evenings, please
complete the form below specifying your
first and second choice of dates to attend.
If we do not hear from you, we will
assume that your films are no longer
outstanding and will cancel your enquiry.

Yours faithfully,

FILMEX PROCESSING LABORATORY

[illegible signature]

Customer Services

As readers, we assume that the Filmex employee has put into the letter all
the facts he wants me to be aware of and in the order in which he believes I
would need to read them. If you decomposed the text into the form it
might have taken in a telephone conversation, you might end up with
something like Example 8.2.

*Example 8.2*

| | |
|---|---|
| TL | Hello? |
| FS | Dr Lynch? |
| TL | Yes. |
| FS | This is Felix Scribe from the Filmex Laboratory. |
| TL | Oh? |
| FS | I'm calling in response to the correspondence about your film. |
| TL | But that was months ago. Why are you ringing me now? |
| FS | Well, as you may know, at the moment we get about 50 films per week without either a return address or where the return address has become separated on the way to our Laboratory. |
| TL | Have you found my film, then? |
| FS | No, we've had a good look through all the unclaimed films but haven't been able to match any of them with yours. |
| TL | So what are you going to do about it? |
| FS | Well, from Monday 28 November to Thursday 1 December 1994, we'll be holding a series of open evenings so that all customers can have a look for themselves at all the unclaimed films to try and find their own missing film. |
| TL | At what time? |
| FS | We'd like people to come between 6.00 p.m. and 7.00 p.m., have a tour of our laboratory, and then look through the outstanding films. We'll be serving light refreshments and giving people the chance to discuss any queries with our technical staff. |

**TL**  How do I apply?

**FS**  If you would like to come to one of these open evenings, we're sending out a form for you to tell us your first and second choice of dates.

**TL**  Thank you. I'll think about it.

**FS**  Thank you. Goodbye.

**TL**  Goodbye.

Decomposing a text in this way highlights for learners the process by which the writer takes decisions both about what information to give the reader (as we saw in the Hemingway text in Chapter 7), in how much detail, and in what order. It also offers one effective way of raising their awareness of the differences between the styles of written and spoken language.

# Classroom writing: the role of the reader

In the case of the Hemingway text (page 130), learners worked on a text that was already available in draft form, but needed adaptation or editing for a particular reader. Text modification is one step removed from writing, since the learners are asked to work on someone else's text. The logical next step is to create classroom tasks that allow learners to make choices of content and form themselves. One way of doing this more interactively is to ask learners to compose a text for a *specific* reader, who can then respond and comment on those choices. It is to that aspect of classroom writing that I turn in this section.

For many generations of learners the question 'Who am I writing for?' had only one answer: the teacher. But a language teacher tends to be a peculiar sort of reader, one who reads in order to identify errors, to evaluate, and perhaps to mark (like the 'judge' role of the listener, which I mentioned in Chapter 5). But in the world outside the classroom, readers read primarily for information or entertainment, rather than to spot language mistakes or to assign a score or grade.

In real-life writing, having a clear picture of our audience or readership is crucial to the success of a piece of writing. However, as Ann Johns of the University of Michigan has argued, of the many aspects of foreign language writing, the one that has received the least attention is the effect of the intended audience (Johns 1993). To become successful writers our students need to develop a sense of audience; this involves understanding who they are writing for, what the readers already know, and what they want and expect to read in the text.

By moving away from the notion that classroom writing is done for the teacher, we can set up interactive writing tasks that exploit the community of readers in the classroom. I would like to illustrate this use of writer–reader interaction with an extract from a pre-writing activity designed to help learners to distinguish between what their reader already knows and what they need to know, in order to make sense of the text the writer intends to write. It comes from the same writing class as Example 4.3 and arose while the learners were working on the following task:

> Think of a technical term in your professional field. Compose a definition or explanation suitable for the other students in your group. See if it is clear and comprehensible to the intended audience. If not, change it.

At the point where we join them, student P (a doctor) is beginning to explain a specialist term to three listeners: two fellow learners, Q (a microbiologist) and R (a vet), and the teacher T. The points requiring the negotiation of meaning in their conversation are underlined in the transcript.

*Example 8.3*

```
P   do you know gall bladder? gall bladder? + gall + bladder +
    maybe you must know + you do you know liver? + + liver
Q   river
P   liver in your body
Q   ah liver                                                    5
P   liver yes + and gall bladder is near liver (gestures) like that
Q   hmhm
P   gall bladder + you know? + it's like that
Q   ah
P   and sometimes many patients suffer from stone in gall      10
    bladder + maybe you
T   can you tell me what the gall bladder does?
P   pardon?
T   can you tell me what the gall bladder does?
P   does?                                                       15
```

T    what is it for?

Q    function

P    ah ah its function is uh almost I must mention about the
     system of uh the solution and + + how to say + + solution
     and the accumulation of deposits                                    20

T    hmhm

P    so liver function to help + liver function to + + + help liver
     function to + + +

R    secret

P    yes secret liquid for digestion for fat                             25

T    ok that's what the liver does + now what does the gall blad-
     der do?

P    so from gall bladder some secretion go to intestine

T    ok

P    and it helps to dissolve lipid + and so especially after taking     30
     some lipodemic food

Q    hm?

T    sorry some what food?

P    lipodemic

T    does that mean fatty?                                               35

P    ah fatty + fatty food

T    sorry 'cause I'm not a doctor + right + fatty food

P    the gall bladder secrets some liquid to solve this food

T    to dissolve it

Q    ah I know                                                           40

T    ok

P    + + not actually but for simple meaning is like so

T    ok

P    so sometimes the stone become in gall bladders so usually
     we must + + it is need to open patient's abdomen to + + take       45
     gall bladder and stone + but now new method uh + so
     laparoscopic cholecystectomy is new method uh + to get off
     gall bladder from patient's body without opening abdomen
     + + ok? + and laparoscopic means we use laparoscopic
     means we use laparoscope and laparoscope is some camera +          50
     or some scope + + do you know gastric camera or
     gastric scope? + + have you ever tried?

Q    no *(laughs)*

P    but you know + do you know? + + yeah + so laparoscopy is
     some camera or scope + + but with more things + and more           55
     things + not so large
     *(shows diameter with her hand)*

T    thinner

P    uh?

T    thinner                                                            60

P  thinner?

Q  thinner

T  or narrower

P  so laparoscopy is to look inside abdomen from outside so uh   65
   we need to open + + uh it's need + it's opened + + we need
   to open small three holes in this abdomen + and each hole is
   within one centimetre + like this + like that + + and from
   one hole is seen scope is inserted inside abdomen + so we
   can find inside of abdomen through TV + +

Q  through TV screen?   70

P  yeah so we we can + cut gall bladder and sew this injury
   with some kind of scissor and <u>hotchkiss</u>

Q  hm?

P  + + you know hotchkiss? + hotchkiss?

T  no we don't know that   75

P  hotchkiss means + + we can use paper

T  scissors?

P  no + clip + uh clip?

T  ah

P  do you know maybe + + many people use like clip with paper   80

Q  paper clip?

P  yeah paper clip + + or paper hotchkiss + um hotchkiss + +
   *(takes two sheets of paper and pinches them together with her
   fingers)* hotchkiss

T  hotchkiss?   85

P  hotchkiss

T  hotchkiss + + I recognize it as a name but I didn't know it
   was a clip

Q  I know clip

P  so maybe most people have ever used + + *(finds a stapled set*   90
   *of papers)* ah ah this is hotchkiss

Q  ah st- + um staple

T  staple

P  staple yes + I'm sorry + in Japan hotchkiss *(laughs)* so with
   scissors and with staple through the other two holes + + so   95
   patients can discharge within one week because we only
   open three holes

T  why do you need to open three holes? + why not just one?

P  so one is to look inside

T  ok   100

P  from outside + + with TV

T  ok

P  and we need two hands to cut + to pick the gall bladder with
   scissors + + and clip + so we need three holes + or
   sometimes four holes   105

> T    how + + you said that the + hole for the scope is one cen-
>        timetre + wide
> P    wide because laparoscopy is + + wide
> T    the diameter
> P    diameter is within one centimetre                              110
> T    ok + how big are the other two holes?
> P    two holes is also one centimetre
> T    really? ok
> P    it's <u>new method</u> + and in Japan usually uh + this new method
>        is + + + held in big hospitals                               115
> T    ok the term that you were defining for us was + the method
>        of doing all that?
> P    yes yes method
> T    can you show us the word + so that we can recognize it
> P    *(shows the words 'laparoscopic cholecystectomy')* <u>laparoscopic</u>  120
>        <u>cholecystectomy</u> + + laparoscopic means we use laparoscope
>        and <u>cholecystectomy</u> means cut off + abdomen
> T    ok
> P    that's all
> (observation data)

I would like to make three comments about that extract. The first point is a general one about the *negotiation of meaning*. Although the participants P, Q, and T were actively engaged in negotiating meaning, learner R contributed only once, when P was trying to explain the function of the liver (line 22). As she paused at 'help liver function to + + +', R suggested 'secret' (in fact he meant 'secrete') and this enabled P to continue. I believe the reason why R did not contribute more to the negotiation is that he did not need to; his own professional field (veterinary medicine) was close to P's, so he was probably familiar with the technique she was explaining.

From the point of view of information distribution in the task (discussed in Chapter 6), it might have been better if the teacher had grouped the students in the class differently, separating people from the same or similar backgrounds. This would have widened the information gap between them and would have encouraged more active negotiation of the meanings that the writers were trying to define. This again underlines how the teacher indirectly contributes to the success of a task by 'managing' the interaction indirectly—through decisions about who should work with whom.

The second point relates to the distinction between *negotiation of content* and *negotiation of meaning*. The learners' conversation was intended not to be an end in itself, but to lead on to the writing-up of an explanation, by giving each learner the chance to assess their audience's knowledge. The relevant knowledge in this case could be of two main types: background and language. Example 8.3 shows that it is not always easy to be certain whether people are negotiating content or meaning. When student P asks 'do you know gall bladder?' at the very beginning of the conversation, she is probably asking whether the others knew the meaning of the English expression, rather than what the gall bladder itself is. On the other hand, her two later questions 'do you know gastric camera or gastric scope? + + have you ever tried?' (lines 51–2) seem to indicate that there P was asking about the listeners' familiarity with the device itself, rather than its English form. One of the important points to be learnt—and for the teacher to make—in this sort of pre-writing activity is that what we assume to be a gap in the listener's vocabulary may in fact be due to lack of background knowledge. In this sort of interaction learners have to be prepared to fill in either type of gap, and also to be sensitive to the difference between the two.

The third point relates to this task as a pre-writing activity. Was it successful? In other words, did student P's conversation with her future readers help her to write a better text? Below is the text that she wrote after the conversation we eavesdropped on in Example 8.3.

### Example 8.4
#### Laparoscopic cholecystectomy
New method to get off gall bladder from patient's body, who suffer from stones in gall bladder. Compared with usual operation, it is need not to open the patient's abdomen. Laparoscope is some scope to look inside abdomen from outside. It's opened three small holes (each is about 1 cm). From one hole a thin scope is inserted inside of abdomen. We can find inside through TV. We can cut and sew gall bladder with some kind of scissors and staples through the other two holes. The patients can discharge within one week.

The main difference between what P said in Example 8.3 and what she wrote in Example 8.4 is the sequence of information, and in particular the position of the technical term she wanted to explain. The sequence of points requiring negotiation in Example 8.3 was this:

> gall bladder—liver—lipodemic—laparoscopic—hotchkiss—
> method—laparoscopic cholecystectomy

Perhaps as a result of hearing the items mentioned in that order, the teacher T was not sure what student P had been defining: 'ok the term that you were defining for us was + the method of doing all that?' (line 116). The first time P had mentioned it (line 47) she did not highlight it enough; it was hidden away in the middle of other information. On the other hand, in her subsequent written text P placed 'laparoscopic cholecystectomy' at the beginning, in the conventional position for the term that is to be defined.

# Classroom writing: the role of the teacher

So far in this chapter I have considered the learner roles of writer and reader, and have looked at ways of exploiting the potential interaction between them. Next I turn to the role of the teacher in organizing classroom writing and in providing feedback on learners' written texts.

Ideas about the teacher's contribution to the development of writing skills have changed a great deal over the past 20 years or so. Until the 1970s the teaching of writing was intended principally to lead to the composition of correct texts. It was concerned with the *product*, with the learner's final written answer. The focus was on accuracy of grammar, vocabulary, spelling, and punctuation—in short, on 'getting it right'.

Since the 1970s, under the influence of North American research in particular, there has been a shift of perspective away from the goal (the final text) and towards the route the writer takes to that goal. In other words, there has been an increasing interest in the *process* of writing. This approach is more concerned with 'going about it the right way'. One of the points that researchers have focused on is to look for possible differences between the writing processes of skilled and unskilled writers, and of people writing in their own and other languages.

Figure 8.1 puts these two perspectives into diagrammatic form; the learner's written text takes on its 'final' shape as a result of the work *en route*. The product can be improved by greater attention to particular aspects of writing (e.g. organization, argument) at an appropriate earlier stage:

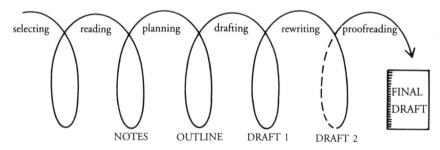

*Figure 8.1: Process and product in writing*

Recently this general view of writing has been expanded to include the notion of *genre*. A genre is a type of text (e.g. recipe, prayer, advertisement), which is recognized as a 'type' by its overall content, structure, and function. The notion of genre is closely connected with that of an audience, and in particular with the idea that readers (and writers) of a specific genre are members of a community of people sharing interests and expectations about its communicative purpose.

One way in which this affects classroom teaching is that differences between genres in different cultures can explain some aspects of learners' performance in the foreign language, as they 'import' conventions from a similar genre in their own language. For example, I have noticed that Japanese learners of English often begin first-contact letters by writing 'Dear Dr Lynch, My name is . . .'. A native writer of English would probably not mention their name in the body of the letter; instead they would leave it to the reader to look to the bottom of the letter to find the name under the signature. On the other hand, they would probably mention their name at the beginning of a different sort of genre, the telephone conversation.

My colleague Miki Inoue tells me that in opening with their name, Japanese writers are transferring into English an equivalent of the phrase *Watashi wa . . . to mōshimasu* ('My name is . . .'), which is used in letters to someone you have not met. So our previous experience of a particular genre can influence not just the way that we express ideas, but also the fact that we choose to mention them at all.

Teaching writing, and providing feedback on learners' texts, requires attention to all three aspects of writing. The sequence in which I have discussed them here reflects the order in which they appeared on the scene. However, from the practical perspective of the classroom teacher, it makes more sense to reverse that order. Considerations of genre should come first because, even before putting pen to paper in response to a task, learners will have formed some idea of the broad shape of the text they should write—e.g. informal letter, recipe, essay, advertisement. Process should come next, because the learners will generate questions to which they need answers as they engage in the process of writing. Attention to product should come last because the editing and correction of the (pre-)final text naturally cannot precede the other two.

This overall movement from genre to process to product is similar to the feedback sequence I suggested in Chapter 6 on speaking: Strategy—Information—Communication—Language. Both emphasize the higher-level issues (topic, structure, and order) and leave attention to bottom-level details until later.

## Activity

### A writing lesson

At this point I would like to pause and consider a writing lesson that I was shown on videotape at a recent teachers' workshop. It was presented as an example of a communicative writing class. It illustrates rather well how a teacher's decisions can influence whether a classroom task leads to interaction—or does not.

The questions I would like you to think about as you read my description of the lesson are these:

1  What did the pupils gain from the writing tasks?
2  What alternative or additional tasks would have made the activity more interactive?

The tape featured a teacher working with a group of about 40 intermediate-level pupils in the ninth year of elementary school, who had been learning English for six years. The topic she had chosen for the lesson was the writing of an informal letter—a genre that the pupils were already familiar with. The context for the task was as follows: a boy of the pupils' age, studying at an English-speaking boarding school, had been given a very negative school report, which had been sent to his parents. The parents, who spoke no English, had shown the report to their eldest son, who translated it for them. They were upset by the boy's performance and asked the elder brother to write a letter admonishing the younger boy for his laziness and urging him to study harder.

Having explained the background, the teacher wrote up the letter from the elder brother, leaving one-word blanks at various points in the text. She then read it aloud to the class and asked the pupils to tell her the missing words. As she was given each correct answer (and she allowed only one) she wrote in the word. When all the blanks had been filled in, she asked the pupils to copy out the entire letter into their exercise books.

Their next task was to produce a reply from the younger brother in which he explained the reasons for his poor report. The teacher wrote up on the board a list of reasons (e.g. noisy study rooms, homesickness, unhelpful teachers). Using this list as a prompt, she then created a letter on the board using sentences composed by the pupils to express the reasons listed on the board. When the letter was complete, the teacher again asked them to copy into their books the entire reply from the younger boy.

As I watched the lesson, I felt that the basic weakness in the teacher's plan was that it did not allow for any interaction between writer and reader. The first letter from the elder brother was wholly the teacher's creation; the second involved some of the pupils as composers of individual sentences, but nobody in the class was required to respond to or comment on the text. For the two texts that the pupils copied from the board there was no reader other than the teacher, whose purpose in reading would probably be to look for any copying slips.

My suggestion for an alternative lesson would start from the same basic situation, but I would divide the class in half: group A would take on the role of 'elder brothers' (or sisters), and group B that of the boarding school pupil. I would ask group A to work in pairs/trios and talk about the criticisms they could make of the younger child's performance, and also the positive reasons they might give him or her for working harder at school. Having planned what to write in the letter, each pupil in group A would then write an individual letter.

Meanwhile I would ask group B, also working in pairs/trios, to adopt the viewpoint of the younger child and to discuss the criticisms and encouragements they expected the older brother or sister to mention. After discussion, group B would each draft a reply to the points they anticipated in the letter.

I would then pair up each group A pupil with a group B partner, to whom the completed letter would be given. The recipient would then read the letter and see to what extent their draft reply has covered the points in the letter from home. Where the older child has raised points that the younger one has not predicted, the draft would then have to be adapted to make it a more adequate response. (Meanwhile, the A group could be working on a suitable exercise on language points arising from their letters.)

Organizing the lesson along these lines would have at least four advantages. Firstly, it would involve all the students in purposeful interaction at the pre-writing pair work stage. Assuming that the learners discussed the letter content in English, they would gain practice in listening to and using spoken English with a specific objective in mind.

Secondly, it would give everyone the chance to put forward and pool their own ideas, independently of the teacher. One drawback of the original lesson was that all the letter content—and most of its language—was produced by the teacher and not the pupils. Apart from giving the learners the communicative initiative, the alternative lesson would allow them to put forward their own ideas, i.e. those of a teenage pupil rather than those of an adult teacher.

Thirdly, it would require the learners to compose a text designed for an audience (the parents) with their own perspective on the issues involved; this should lead to a natural conflict of opinion and so to further communication.

Fourthly, at the point when the letter is handed over by the older child to the younger, the recipients would be reading for a real purpose, since they need to compare the points mentioned in the letter of complaint with those they have anticipated. Any unexpected points appearing in the elder brother's letter have to be responded to by modifying or adding to their draft reply.

The differences between original and alternative writing lessons could be summarized as follows:

| original lesson | alternative lesson |
|---|---|
| Whole class work: teacher-orientated | Pair work: learner-orientated |
| Ideas from teacher: uniform content | Ideas from learners: individual letters |
| Teacher composes: learners copy | Learners compose for specific readers |
| Limited reading | Challenging reading: as input to the letter of response |

*Table 8.1*

Rearranging the task in this way would provide a framework for the inter-action between the individual writer and reader that is a necessary part of any exchange of letters in real life. It requires the learners to take responsibility for what to write (content) as well as how to write it (language). It involves a potentially productive information gap, since the reader cannot be sure what the critical letter will say in detail, but can formulate a response in general terms.

# Feedback during writing

## *Learner-initiated feedback*

One reason why learners should receive feedback and advice from the teacher during the writing process, instead of waiting until they have completed their text, is that it makes sound psychological sense. The doubts and problems that arise during the activity of writing are good opportunities for learning from someone else how to overcome them.

Even when a class of learners are working in parallel on what appears to be the 'same' task, they may have different individual perceptions of what they need assistance with and when. Below is a list of questions (Example 8.5) extracted from an academic writing lesson in which the teacher had decided to reverse the normal classroom roles.

He told the learners that he would respond to whatever questions they individually needed to ask about their current work on the task, but would not do any whole-group teaching. Each student was free to decide which area they wanted the teacher's help with or comments on—rather like the indirect negotiation listening task described in Chapter 5. The ten questions shown in Example 8.5 were asked by different students.

*Example 8.5*
1  So there's no need to quantify? This is the point I wanted to ask.
2  Is it correct in the introduction to give him *(the reader)* a clue?
3  Present tense here?
4  Do you know about statistics? . . . our difficulty is to interpret these results in terms of good English . . . this is why I ask about your statistical knowledge.
5  I am comparing (X and Y) so how can I start my introduction?
6  I would like to ask one thing. What would be the better start: to give the country background or to give the importance of the seed?
7  Is this clear what I have written?
8  Could you please read it and tell me my errors?
9  I want to emphasize 'legumes' here. Can you show me how to?
10 Sometimes you find a writer has referred another writer. How are we going to quote in the text?

Notice the variety of the issues on which the students asked for feedback: content (questions 1 and 2), uncertainties over grammar (question 3) and vocabulary (question 4), balance (question 5), organization and sequence (question 6), clarity (question 7), information focus (question 9), and register (question 10).

By adopting this approach, the teacher was moving away from the traditional form of post-writing feedback on written work. Often we have in mind one particular 'teaching point' and so tend to focus exclusively on correcting that point; but, as Example 8.5 shows, letting the learners ask for assistance with whatever is currently an obstacle to their writing provides potential opportunities for learning. They notice a gap for themselves; what they want from the teacher is the information to fill it.

# Feedback after writing

## Clarification requests

In Chapter 4 I mentioned research that found that in the case of spoken interaction it can be more effective for teachers to use implicit negative feedback, such as clarification requests, than to correct learners' speech errors explicitly (Nobuyoshi and Ellis 1993). Similarly, there is some evidence from the teaching of writing in the first language (Knoblauch and Brannon 1981) and the foreign language (Sheppard 1992) that marking errors on students' texts leads to less improvement in writing than asking the writer to explain points that are unclear in their draft.

These questions can come from teacher or fellow learner, or both. The series of three Examples below (8.6 to 8.8) show how a Japanese learner of English gradually refined a text in response to clarification requests, first from another student and then from her teacher. She was taking an intermediate-level class preparing for university study in Britain. The students were asked to compose a text about a traditional event or ceremony in their home culture for a reader from another culture. Example 8.6 is the Japanese learner's first draft about the festival of Hanami.

*Example 8.6*

Hanami

In the season of cherry blossoms—around early April when it is warm and comfortable to stay outside, some Japanese people have a party under cherry trees to enjoy the flowers, and others visit temples, parks, or some places which are famous for beautiful cherry blossoms. These are called *hanami* in Japanese.

Cherry blossom is an important flower for Japanese. Because school begins on April, Japanese people think that cherry blossom symbolize a kind of new year. Because Japanese cherry blossoms are so beautiful and their period is so short that Japanese people wish their lives could be same as them. That's means in Japan it is disgraceful to cling to something—post, money, life—with a bad grace.

The first person to read the text was an Arabic-speaking learner. He seemed to have no problems with the first paragraph, but could not understand the relationship between the first and last sentences in the second paragraph. The writer's response to his queries was to make clearer the cultural and philosophical associations of cherry blossom. One of the effects of expanding that element of her text was that she felt she needed to divide the original second paragraph into two. Example 8.7 shows the revised text (with the main changes underlined).

*Example 8.7*

Japanese people love cherry blossom. For example it is a symbol of the new pupils, because school start from April, and a symbol of fine sensibility. In Japan nothing can be eternal. The shape of nature changes quickly. Because Japanese houses made from wood, they can not be long. Japanese people love the feeling of fine sensibility.

Some Japanese people wish their lives could be same as the flower—not only the bloom is very beautiful but also the ending is noble. That means the ending of life is important in Japan. It is disgraceful to persist on position, money and life.

She showed the revised text to the same reader, who confirmed that it had now clarified the point he had found vague before. She then passed the text on to the teacher, who felt that 'fine sensibility' was archaic and suggested 'sensitivity'. He also thought that the adjective 'disgraceful' was not quite appropriate in this context. The writer took her text away again and then produced the final version below:

*Example 8.8*

> Japanese people love cherry blossom. For example it is a symbol of the new pupils, because school starts from April, and also <u>a symbol of the beauty of impermanence and the sensitive heart capable of appreciating beauty</u>—*mono no aware*. In Japan nothing can be eternal. The shape of nature changes quickly. Because Japanese buildings made from wood, they can not last long. Japanese people love the feeling.
>
> Some Japanese people wish their lives could be same as the flower—not only is the bloom very beautiful but also the ending is noble. That means the ending of life is important in Japan. It is <u>shameful that dying people still hang on to job, money and life</u>.

That final version is interesting because it shows how the feedback from two readers—a fellow learner and the teacher—have led the writer to realize the difficulty of finding a precise equivalent for—*mono no aware*, the Japanese thought which lay behind her text. Example 8.8 therefore includes both the original expression and her paraphrase for it in English.

The conclusion usually drawn from research into the effectiveness of feedback to learners is not that we should give up the idea of correcting learners, but that we need to develop ways of making feedback more effective. It could be that particular sorts of error are more successfully highlighted (and remembered) in certain ways, or that particular techniques of correction suit different types or levels of learner. One practical solution is to offer learners a range of feedback types: a combination of learner and teacher comments and clarification requests and corrections, such as illustrated here, may stand a greater chance of success than reliance on a single technique.

# Summary

In this chapter I have explored the pedagogic potential of viewing writing as an interactive language process. I have presented some of the practical implications of emphasizing the negotiation of meaning between writer and reader—either the potential reader (at the composing stage) or the actual reader (who can provide feedback after a draft is complete).

Feedback from both fellow learners and the teacher helps to sensitize the learner-writer to the importance of bearing in mind the reader's knowledge, interests, and needs when composing a text. As I have stressed, teachers should think of writing as a form of communication that demands interactive skills similar to those of speaking. Interaction before, during, and after writing will make learners more effective writers.

## *Suggestions for further reading*

### *Teaching writing (general)*

**Hedge, T.** 1988. *Writing.* Oxford: Oxford University Press. A useful source of ideas about and suggestions for the teaching of writing.

**Kroll, B.** (ed.). 1990. *Second Language Writing.* Cambridge: Cambridge University Press. This is a collection of research-based articles dealing mainly with learners writing for academic purposes.

### *Process-oriented writing*

**White, R.** and **V. Arndt.** 1991. *Process Writing.* London: Longman. The authors summarize historical trends in the teaching of writing and provide plenty of examples of classroom tasks emphasizing the components of the writing process.

### *Reader-oriented writing*

**Burbidge, N., P. Gray, S. Levy.** and **M. Rinvolucri.** 1996. *Letters.* Oxford: Oxford University Press. A lively compendium of classroom tasks exploiting the interactive dimension of letter-writing (and letter-reading).

### *Feedback*

Two papers from Barbara Kroll's collection (details above) deal with issues of teacher feedback on learners' writing: how, when, why, and with what results.

**Cohen, A.** and **M. Cavalcanti.** 1990. 'Feedback on compositions: teacher and student verbal reports.' pp. 155–77.

**Leki, I.** 1990. 'Coaching from the margins: issues in written response.' pp. 57–68.

### *Genre*

**Swales, J.** 1990. *Genre Analysis.* Cambridge: Cambridge University Press. This book provides a detailed treatment of the notion of genre, applying it to English for academic purposes.

**Wallace, C.** 1992. *Reading.* Oxford: Oxford University Press. This includes a practical introduction to genre and relates it to the teaching of reading in a general English context.

# 9 POSTSCRIPT

## Four reasons for not changing anything

In my introduction I said you might find yourself thinking 'it wouldn't work here because . . .'. In this final section I discuss four possible objections to the shift towards more interactive tasks proposed in this book.

### 'We don't have the resources'

From working in Brazil, India, and Malaysia I am very aware that in Edinburgh I teach in relative comfort and with access to a wide variety of teaching aids. But in writing this book I have assumed that the teachers and trainers reading it have access to relatively limited resources: duplicating equipment such as a photocopier, and an audio-cassette recorder/player.

Of course, if you do have more advanced electronic equipment at your disposal, then you will be able to adapt some of the tasks I have described. For example, the interactive letter writing activity in Chapter 8 could be transformed into one in which learners in different places correspond by e-mail, rather than exchanging paper messages in the same classroom.

The indirect negotiation task described in Chapter 5 on listening would be well suited to an interactive video laboratory. In the classroom version, the learners resolve their current comprehension by choosing one of four options:

1 hearing the problematic section again
2 seeing whether the next part of the text will help
3 asking the teacher for more information
4 seeing whether any other listener has worked out the meaning.

In an interactive video version, the learner could have various additional forms of visual support: slowed replay, replay with English subtitles, replay with translation, and so on.

In the section on 'interaction about texts' in Chapter 7 I described how when learners discuss problematic points in a reading text, they may end up exploring areas of language knowledge, personal experiences, background knowledge, and cultural assumptions, among other things. If you have access to multimedia computers, then you could create reading comprehension texts which the learner reads on screen, with the option of consulting an electronic dictionary (for help with language problems), a CD encyclopedia (for background information), and even a set of cultural notes that you have prepared on specific points mentioned in the text.

However, for most of us these electronic devices are a distant possibility rather than current reality. (It is also worth stressing that high technology is not necessarily a good thing; unless it is used carefully, the computer actually brings the risk of *reducing* interaction between learners, not increasing it.)

But the tasks I have described in the book are within the material resources of the majority of teachers. More important than the practical details of each task is the underlying *principle* of creating more opportunities for learners to engage in real interaction—and this can be done without sophisticated electronics.

## 'Our classes are too large for interaction'

Obviously class size can be a key influence on your decisions about what is feasible in the classroom, but there are ways of getting round the numbers problem. Once we have accepted that there are positive benefits to be gained from introducing more interactive work, then it becomes a question of making that manageable with the size of class we are working with. For example, if your solution is to use group work, then you—and the students—will have to accept that you will not be able to listen in to every group all the time. But group work is not the only way to encourage interaction; in Chapter 4 I mentioned Karuna Kumar's article, which describes a secondary school teacher organizing whole-class interaction with a relatively large class (45 pupils) and still managing to create opportunities for the learners to contribute ideas and to make creative use of their English.

## 'Our students don't expect to be taught that way'

Let me deal first with 'that way'. This book has explored the role of interaction-oriented tasks as *one part* of learners' classroom experience of the target language. I have not argued for an exclusively communicative 'method'. To give you an idea of how the balance might work out in practice, in the course I am currently teaching we spend about half the class time on group interaction of various kinds, and the other half on individual reading/writing and on whole-class activities (e.g. grammatical exercises) led by the teacher.

The issue of expectations is important. For most of my students, inter-active tasks that de-emphasize the role of the teacher are a novelty. In their previous language learning the teacher has usually assumed the tra-ditional dominant role. But it does not take long for the learners to adjust their expectations. Here are the comments of one student writing about her first three weeks in a class that included interaction-based writing (like that in the section on clarification requests in Chapter 8):

> In the beginning of the course I was not used to talk with fellow students, especially the topics not related to my subject. I always waited for a 'correct' answer and felt getting nothing from discus-sion. However, things I dislike returned to the things I like after I found the advantages similar to discussing with the teacher. However, it was difficult to get exactly correct grammar or vocabularies from peer evaluation sometimes. Therefore about those in writing I pre-fer getting information from tutors to from peers, although I like brainstorming.

She has summed up the situation very well, I think. She finds that inter-action with other learners is valuable for some aspects of writing (gener-ating ideas and organizing content), but that interaction with the teacher is a better source of feedback on the accuracy of her English. What is required is a balance between the two types of classroom experience.

## 'We haven't been trained to teach like this'

Neither have I! Although initial teacher training has become more com-municatively orientated since I started teaching in 1970, it is still unusual for trainees to be asked to analyse how conversations work, and in par-ticular conversations involving one or more learners of the language. Even if there is some discussion of these issues, the main emphasis in training courses remains on texts featuring native speakers. One of the aims of this book is to raise trainees' awareness of the characteristics of interaction, and give them a more realistic picture of what to expect in the classroom.

Apart from the need to familiarize trainees with the sort of language *prod-uct* to expect from learners in the classroom, there is an important issue of *process*: the roles of teachers and learners. I have argued that learners should take—that is, that we should allow and encourage them to take—the communicative initiative more often. I recognize that this has to be done carefully, and in a way that is compatible with local educational norms and traditions; above all it must not be seen by teachers or any-one else as 'a threat to instructional management' (Johnson 1992: 530).

In case you think that the idea of giving learners greater responsibility is appropriate only to the 'Western' humanistic tradition (and in small classes of adult learners), here is the view of an Indian teacher trainer:

> [Learners] will not learn unless they enjoy the learning and attempts are made by the teachers to involve them in the process of learning. This is possible only when the teachers give up the teaching mode, share the learner's concerns, allow them to contribute to learning and recognize their contributions. The teachers, therefore, should . . . become co-participants, helpers, friends in the process of learning.
> (Kundu 1993: 4)

Those are the words not of a trainer working at a privileged university in the developed world, but one involved in the education of tribal learners at rural secondary schools in Orissa, one of the most disadvantaged states in India. If more interaction, and more equal interaction, has been found feasible and valuable there—in large classes and in a culture with a strong tradition of respect for the authority of the teacher—we can surely make it work elsewhere.

# GLOSSARY

I have included in this glossary only those items which have a special or technical meaning in the learning and teaching of languages. The definitions reflect the terms as used in the book. Other writers may use them in different ways.

*accessible:* Understandable in terms of both expression and content.

*accommodation:* Refers to the way in which (in our first language) we adjust what we say and how we say it according to our relationship with the person we are talking to. See also *simplification.*

*adjustment:* The way(s) in which speakers alter what they say in order to make it understandable to their audience.

*affective:* To do with an individual's emotional response to some aspect of learning. Often contrasted with the *cognitive* or intellectual dimension.

*assumed knowledge:* Information that a speaker or writer takes for granted when communicating.

*behavioural strategies (interactive strategies):* Interactional devices that a listener can use to solve a current listening problem, such as asking for clarification or repetition.

*bottom-up processing:* Step-by-step decoding of a text, beginning with the smallest linguistic elements (sounds or letters) and gradually building up larger units of meaning. Contrasted with *top-down* and *interactive processing.*

*cognitive:* To do with a person's intellectual processes in understanding a message.

*comprehensible input:* Message including linguistic items which are above a learner's current proficiency level, but can be understood by using contextual clues and background knowledge.

*Comprehensible Output Hypothesis:* Theory that learners make progress by engaging in communicative activities in which they are 'pushed' (by listeners' difficulties in understanding them) to make their production more native-like and comprehensible. Associated with Merrill Swain.

*co-text:* The other parts of a text preceding and following the item currently being processed.

*decomposition:* The 'conversion' of a written text into a question-and-answer dialogue which represents a possible 'parallel' spoken version of the written content.

*display question (test question, pedagogic question):* A question to which the asker already knows the answer.

*elaborative simplification:* Process (or effect) of making a text more accessible by providing additional information, such as explanations or examples. Used in contrast to *restrictive simplification*.

*Foreigner Talk:* Term used to describe the linguistic features of speech addressed to non-native listeners. Associated with early input studies.

*Foreigner Talk Discourse:* Conversation characteristic of native–non-native communication, viewed in terms of both input and interaction adjustments.

*genre:* A type of text, recognizable by its form and function: for example, a thank-you letter or a recipe.

*input:* Messages (spoken or written) addressed to the learner.

*Input Hypothesis:* Theory that learners acquire a second language principally (or solely) by understanding messages in it (especially *comprehensible input*). Associated with Stephen Krashen.

*interaction:* Reciprocal communication, normally spoken, to which both (or all) participants actively contribute.

*interactive processing:* Comprehension using information from multiple sources, combining *top-down* and *bottom-up* routes.

*linguistic simplification:* see *restrictive simpification*.

*mental model:* The listener's (reader's) current internal picture of the message a speaker (writer) is trying to convey.

*modification:* The process of simplifying a text, or a change made in that process, especially in the case of spoken communication.

*negotiation of content:* Process by which learners reach agreement about what they have heard or read.

*negotiation of meaning:* The mutual process by which participants try to ensure that they understand (and are understood by) each other, by means of comprehension checks, clarification requests, and so on.

*noticeable:* An item is made noticeable if the learner's conscious attention is focused on its form, function, or meaning.

*noticing the gap:* Becoming aware of the difference between your own (or another learner's) performance and that of a native user of the language.

*on-line modification:* An adjustment made by a speaker to a message as he/she is in the process of speaking, normally in response to a problem signalled by the listener. Used in contrast with *pre-* and *post-modification.*

*optional information exchange task (one-way task):* A classroom task whose completion does not depend on all the partners contributing to the interaction.

*post-modification:* Adjustment made to a tape recording or written text to make it easier for learners to understand, e.g. editing the tape or adding marginal notes to a reading passage.

*pragmatic meaning:* The 'real' or full meaning of a message; what the original listener or reader was intended to understand, in that particular context and in the light of their particular knowledge.

*pre-modification:* Planned or scripted adjustments to a pedagogic text (spoken or written) in the interest of *simplification.*

*psycholinguistic strategies (internal strategies):* Mental 'actions' taken by a listener or reader to deal with a comprehension problem, e.g. guessing at the meaning of an unknown item. Used in contrast with *behavioural* or *interactive strategies.*

*pushdown:* A 'pause' in a conversation while the participants try to *repair* (resolve) a communication problem; particularly common in interaction between native and non-native speakers of a language.

*real question (referential question, genuine question):* A question to which the asker does not know the answer. Contrasted with *display question.*

*reformulation:* Rephrasing something in a way that makes it more accessible to the listener or reader.

*repair:* The process by which partners remedy comprehension problems in conversation.

*required information exchange task (two-way task):* A classroom activity designed so that every member of a group has to contribute if the task is to be completed satisfactorily, e.g. a jigsaw speaking task.

*restrictive simplification (linguistic simplification):* Making a text more accessible by restricting the range and complexity of the language used. Used in contrast to *elaborative simplification.*

*simplification:* (1) Process of making a text more accessible; or (2) means employed to achieve greater access; or (3) the effect of (1) or (2).

'*Teacher Talk*': Stereotype (or caricature) of the way teachers are thought to modify their speech to communicate with low-proficiency learners. In fact, teacher–learner *interaction* differs from other forms of speech mainly in terms of quantity rather than quality of *modification*.

*top-down processing:* Using higher-level information, such as expectations and topic knowledge, to construct an interpretation of an incoming message. Contrasted with *bottom-up processing*; see also *interactive processing*.

# BIBLIOGRAPHY

**Allwright, R.** 1984. 'The analysis of discourse in interlanguage studies: the pedagogical evidence' in A. Davies, C. Criper, and A. Howatt (eds.): *Interlanguage.* Edinburgh: Edinburgh University Press. pp. 204–22.

**Anderson, A.** and **T. Lynch.** 1988. *Listening.* Oxford: Oxford University Press.

**Arthur, B., R. Weiner, M. Culver, Y. J. Lee,** and **D. Thomas.** 1980. 'The register of impersonal discourse to foreigners: verbal adjustments to foreign accent' in D. Larsen-Freeman (ed.): *Discourse Analysis in Second Language Research.* Rowley, Mass.: Newbury House. pp. 111–24.

**Aston, G.** 1986. 'Trouble-shooting in interaction: the more the merrier?' *Applied Linguistics* 7/2: 128–43.

**Brock, C.** 1984. 'The effects of referential questions on ESL classroom discourse.' *TESOL Quarterly* 20/1: 47–59.

**Brown, G.** 1986. 'Investigating listening comprehension in context' *Applied Linguistics* 7/3: 284–302.

**Brown, G.** 1990. *Listening to Spoken English.* (2nd edition). London: Longman.

**Brown, G.** and **G. Yule.** 1983. *Discourse Analysis.* Cambridge: Cambridge University Press.

**Burbidge, N., P. Gray, S. Levy,** and **M. Rinvolucri.** 1996. *Letters.* Oxford: Oxford University Press.

**Bygate, M.** 1987. *Speaking.* Oxford: Oxford University Press.

**Carrell, P.** 1987. 'Content and formal schemata in ESL reading.' *TESOL Quarterly* 21/3: 461–82.

**Carrell, P., J. Devine,** and **D. Eskey.** (eds.). 1988. *Interactive Approaches to Second Language Reading.* Cambridge: Cambridge University Press.

**Cervantes, R.** 1983. 'Say it Again, Sam: The Effect of Exact Repetition on Listening Comprehension.' Term paper, University of Hawaii at Manoa.

**Cervantes, R.** and **G. Gainer.** 1992. 'The effects of syntactic simplification and repetition on listening comprehension.' *TESOL Quarterly* 26/4: 767–70.

**Chaudron, C.** 1979. 'Complexity of ESL teachers' speech and vocabulary explanation/elaboration.' Paper presented at TESOL Convention, Boston 1979.

**Chaudron, C.** 1983. 'Simplification of input: topic reinstatements and their effects on L2 learners' recognition and recall.' *TESOL Quarterly* 17/3: 437–58.

**Chaudron, C.** 1988. *Second Language Classrooms.* Cambridge: Cambridge University Press.

**Chiang, C. S.** and **P. Dunkel.** 1992. 'The effect of speech modification, prior knowledge and listening proficiency on EFL lecture learning.' *TESOL Quarterly* 26/2: 345–74.

**Clarke, M.** 1994. 'The dysfunctions of the theory/practice discourse.' *TESOL Quarterly* 28/1: 9–26.

**Cohen, A.** and **M. Cavalcanti.** 1990. 'Feedback on compositions: teacher and student verbal reports' in Kroll (ed.). 1990: 155–77.

**Cook, G.** 1989. *Discourse.* Oxford: Oxford University Press.

**Corder, S. P.** 1981. *Error Analysis and Interlanguage.* Oxford: Oxford University Press.

**Cotterall, S.** 1990. 'Developing reading strategies through small-group interaction.' *RELC Journal* 21/2: 55–69.

**Dahl, D.** 1981. 'The role of experience in speech modifications for second-language learners.' *Minnesota Papers in Linguistics and Philosophy of Language* 7: 216–32.

**Davies, A.** 1984. 'Simple, simplified and simplification: what is authentic?' in J. C. Alderson and A. H. Urquhart (eds.): *Reading in a Foreign Language.* London: Longman. pp. 181–98.

**Davies, A.** and **H. G. Widdowson.** 1974. 'Reading and writing' in J. P. B. Allen and S. P. Corder (eds.): *Techniques in Applied Linguistics.* Oxford: Oxford University Press. pp. 155–201.

**Day, R.** (ed.). 1986. *Talking to Learn: Conversation in Second Language Acquisition.* Rowley, Mass.: Newbury House.

**Derwing, T.** 1989. 'Information type and its relation to nonnative speaker comprehension.' *Language Learning* 39/2: 157–73.

**Doughty, C.** and **T. Pica.** 1986. '"Information gap" tasks: do they facilitate second language acquisition?' *TESOL Quarterly* 20/2: 305–25.

**Ellis, R.** 1985. *Understanding Second Language Acquisition.* Oxford: Oxford University Press.

**Ellis, R.** 1994. *The Study of Second Language Acquisition.* Oxford: Oxford University Press.

*Englisch für berufsbildende Schulen: Grundlehrgang.* 1975. Munich: Hüber Holzmann.

**Færch, C.** 1981. 'Inferencing procedures and communication strategies in lexical comprehension.' Paper presented at BAAL Seminar on Interpretive Strategies in Language Learning, University of Lancaster, September 1981.

**Ferguson, C.** 1971. 'Absence of copula and the notion of simplicity: a study of normal speech, baby talk, foreigner talk and pidgins' in D. Hymes (ed.): *Pidginization and Creolization of Languages.* New York: Cambridge University Press.

**Gass, S.** and **C. Madden** (eds.). 1985. *Input in Second Language Acquisition.* Rowley, Mass.: Newbury House.

**Griffiths, R.** 1990. 'Speech rate and NNS comprehension: a preliminary study.' *Language Learning* 40/3: 311–36.

**Harder, P.** 1981. 'Discourse as self-expression: On the reduced personality of the second-language learner.' *Applied Linguistics* 1/3: 262–70.

**Hawkins, B.** 1985. 'Is an "appropriate response" always so appropriate?' in Gass and Madden (eds.). 1985: 162–78.

**Heaton, J. B.** 1966. *Composition through Pictures.* London: Longman.

**Hedge, T.** 1988. *Writing.* Oxford: Oxford University Press.

**Honeyfield, J.** 1977. 'Simplification.' *TESOL Quarterly* 11/4: 431–40.

**Johns, A.** 1993. 'Written argumentation for real audiences: Suggestions for teacher research and classroom practice.' *TESOL Quarterly* 27/1: 75–90.

**Johnson, K.** 1992. 'Learning to teach: Instructional actions and decisions of pre-service ESL teachers.' *TESOL Quarterly* 26/3: 507–35.

**Johnson, K.** 1995. *Understanding Communication in Second Language Classrooms.* Cambridge: Cambridge University Press.

**Johnson, P.** 1981. 'Effects on reading comprehension of language complexity and cultural background of a text.' *TESOL Quarterly* 15/1: 169–81.

**Johnson, P.** 1982. 'Effects on reading comprehension of building background knowledge.' *TESOL Quarterly* 16/4: 503–16.

**Kasper, G.** 1984. 'Pragmatic comprehension in learner–native speaker discourse.' *Language Learning* 34/1: 1–18.

**Kelch, K.** 1985. 'Modified input as an aid to comprehension.' *Studies in Second Language Acquisition* 7/1: 81–90.

**Knoblauch, C.** and **L. Brannon.** 1981. 'Teacher commentary on students' writing: the state of the art.' *Freshman English News* 10: 1–4.

**Krashen, S.** 1985. *The Input Hypothesis: Issues and Implications.* London: Longman.

**Kroll, B.** (ed.). 1990. *Second Language Writing.* Cambridge: Cambridge University Press.

**Kumar, K.** 1992. 'Does class size really make a difference? Exploring classroom interaction in large and small classes.' *RELC Journal* 23/1: 29–47.

**Kundu, M.** 1993. *Teachers' Handbook for 'Progressive English'.* Bhubaneswar, India: ELT Mov.

**Larsen-Freeman, D.** (ed.). 1980. *Discourse Analysis in Second Language Research.* Rowley, Mass.: Newbury House.

**Leki, I.** 1990. 'Coaching from the margins: issues in written response' in Kroll (ed.). 1990: 57–68.

**Lightbown, P.** and **N. Spada.** 1993. *How Languages are Learned.* Oxford: Oxford University Press.

**Long, M.** 1981. 'Variation in Linguistic Input for Second Language Acquisition.' Paper presented at the European–North American Workshop on Cross-Linguistic SLA Research, Lake Arrowhead, California, September 1981.

**Long, M.** 1983. 'Linguistic and conversational adjustments to non-native speakers.' *Studies in Second Language Acquisition* 5/2: 177–93.

**Long, M.** 1985. 'Input and second language acquisition theory' in Gass and Madden (eds.). 1985: 337–93.

**Long, M., L. Adams, M. Maclean,** and **F. Castanos.** 1976. 'Doing things with words: verbal interaction in lockstep and small group classroom situations' in J. Fanselow and R. Crymes (eds.): *On TESOL '76.* Washington, D.C.: TESOL. pp. 137–563.

**Long, M.** and **C. Sato.** 1983. 'Classroom foreigner talk discourse: forms and functions of teachers' questions' in Seliger and Long (eds.). 1983: 268–86.

**Luk, V.** 1994. 'Developing Interactional Listening Strategies in a Foreign Language: A Study of Two Classroom Approaches.' Ph.D. dissertation, University of Edinburgh, Scotland.

**Lynch, A.** 1988a. 'Grading Foreign Language Listening Comprehension Materials: The Use of Naturally Modified Interaction.' Ph.D. dissertation, University of Edinburgh, Scotland.

**Lynch, A.** 1988b. 'Speaking up or talking down: foreign learners' reactions to teacher talk.' *ELT Journal* 42/2: 109–16.

**Lynch, T.** 1986. 'Modifications to foreign listeners: the stories teachers tell.' *ERIC Document ED 274 225.* Washington, D.C.: Center for Applied Linguistics.

**Lynch, T.** 1987. 'Using on-line listening comprehension.' Paper presented at TESOL Scotland Conference, Stirling, Scotland, November 1987.

**Lynch, T.** 1991. 'Questioning roles in the classroom.' *English Language Teaching Journal* 45/3: 201–10.

**Lynch, T.** and **K. Anderson.** 1992. *Study Speaking.* Cambridge: Cambridge University Press.

**Malamah-Thomas, A.** 1987. *Classroom Interaction.* Oxford: Oxford University Press.

**McGregor, G.** 1986. 'Listening outside the participation framework' in G. McGregor and R. White (eds.): *The Art of Listening.* London: Croom Helm. pp. 55–72.

**Moncur, A.** 1994. 'Passion of men in blameless trousers.' *Observer* 31 July 1994.

**Nobuyoshi, J.** and **R. Ellis.** 1993. 'Focused communication tasks and second language acquisition.' *ELT Journal* 47/3: 203–10.

**Nolasco, R.** and **L. Arthur.** 1987. *Conversation.* Oxford: Oxford University Press.

**Nunan, D.** 1989. *Designing Tasks for the Communicative Classroom.* Cambridge: Cambridge University Press.

**Nuttall, C.** 1982. *Teaching Reading Skills in a Foreign Language.* London: Heinemann.

**O'Neill, R.** and **R. Scott.** 1974. *Viewpoints.* London: Longman.

**Parkinson, B.** 1986. 'Classroom Processes.' Lecture materials, Department of Applied Linguistics, University of Edinburgh, Scotland.

**Pica, T.** 1987. 'Second language acquisition, social interaction, and the classroom.' *Applied Linguistics* 8/1: 3–21.

**Pica, T.** 1988. 'Interlanguage adjustments as an outcome of NS–NNS negotiated interaction.' *Language Learning* 38/1: 45–73.

**Pica, T.** 1991. 'Classroom interaction, negotiation and comprehension: redefining relationships.' *System* 19/4: 437–52.

**Pica, T.** 1994. 'Research on negotiation: What does it reveal about second-language learning conditions, processes, and outcomes?' *Language Learning* 44/3: 493–527.

**Pica, T., L. Holliday, N. Lewis,** and **L. Morgenthaler.** 1989. 'Comprehensible output as an outcome of linguistic demands on the learner.' *Studies in Second Language Acquisition* 11/1: 63–90.

**Pica, T., R. Young,** and **C. Doughty.** 1987. 'The impact of interaction on comprehension.' *TESOL Quarterly* 21/4: 737–58.

**Porter, P.** 1986. 'How learners talk to each other: input and interaction in task-centered discussions' in Day (ed.). 1986: 200–22.

**Rost, M.** 1990. *Listening in Language Learning.* London: Longman.

**Rost, M.** and **S. Ross.** 1991. 'Learner use of strategies in interaction: typology and teachability.' *Language Learning* 41/2: 235–73.

**Rulon, K.** and **J. McCreary.** 1986. 'Negotiation of content: teacher-fronted and small-group interaction' in Day (ed.). 1986: 182–99.

**Schachter, J.** 1983. 'Nutritional needs of language learners' in M. Clarke and J. Handscombe (eds.): *On TESOL '82: Pacific Perspectives on Language Learning and Teaching.* Washington, D.C.: TESOL. pp. 175–89.

**Schegloff, E.** 1979. 'The relevance of repair to syntax-for-conversation' in T. Givón (ed.): *Syntax and Semantics Volume 12: Discourse and Syntax.* New York: Academic Press. pp. 261–86.

**Schegloff, E., G. Jefferson,** and **H. Sacks.** 1977. 'The preference for self-correction in the organization of repair in conversation.' *Language* 53: 361–82.

**Schmidt, R.** 1990. 'The role of consciousness in second language learning.' *Applied Linguistics* 11/2: 129–58.

**Schwartz, J.** 1980. 'The negotiation of meaning: repair in conversations between second language learners of English' in Larsen-Freeman (ed.). 1980: 138–53.

**Schwerdtfeger, I.** 1983. 'Foreigner talk: implications for foreign language teaching.' *Nottingham Circular in Applied Linguistics.* December 1983: 141–58.

**Scottish Education Department.** 1984. Listening Comprehension Project: Training Materials. Edinburgh, Scotland: University of Edinburgh.

**Sharwood Smith, M.** 1981. 'Consciousness-raising and the second language learner.' *Applied Linguistics* 2/2: 159–68.

**Shehadeh, A.** 1991. 'Comprehension and Performance in Second Language Acquisition: A Study of Second Language Learners' Production of Modified Comprehensible Output.' Ph.D. dissertation, University of Durham, England.

**Sheppard, K.** 1992. 'Two feedback types: Do they make a difference?' *RELC Journal* 23/1: 104–10.

**Sinclair, J.** and **M. Coulthard.** 1975. *Towards an Analysis of Discourse.* Oxford: Oxford University Press.

**Slimani, A.** 1992. 'Evaluation of classroom interaction' in J. C. Alderson and A. Beretta (eds.): *Evaluating Second Language Education.* Cambridge: Cambridge University Press. pp. 197–220.

**Swain, M.** 1985. 'Communicative competence: some roles of comprehensible input and comprehensible output in its development' in Gass and Madden (eds.). 1985: 235–53.

**Swales, J.** 1990. *Genre Analysis.* Cambridge: Cambridge University Press.

**Varonis, E.** and **S. Gass.** 1985. 'Non-native–non-native conversation: a model for the negotiation of meaning.' *Applied Linguistics* 6/1: 71–90.

**Wallace, C.** 1992. *Reading.* Oxford: Oxford University Press.

**West, M.** 1955. *Learning to Read a Foreign Language.* London: Longman.

**Whitaker, S.** 1983. 'Comprehension questions: about face!' *ELT Journal* 37/4: 329–34.

**White, L.** 1987. 'Against comprehensible input: the Input Hypothesis and the development of L2 competence.' *Applied Linguistics* 9/2: 261–85.

**White, R.** and **V. Arndt.** 1991. *Process Writing.* London: Longman.

**Widdowson, H. G.** 1978. *Teaching Language as Communication.* Oxford: Oxford University Press.

**Widdowson, H. G.** 1979. *Exploration in Applied Linguistics.* Oxford: Oxford University Press.

**Widdowson, H. G.** 1990. *Aspects of Language Teaching.* Oxford: Oxford University Press.

**Wymer, N.** 1973. *The Kon-Tiki Expedition.* London: Longman.

**Yule, G.** 1990. 'Interactive conflict resolution in English.' *World Englishes* 9: 53–62.

**Yule, G.** 1991. 'Developing communicative effectiveness through the negotiated resolution of referential conflicts.' *Linguistics and Education* 3: 31–45.

**Yule, G.** 1994. 'ITAs, interaction and communicative effectiveness' in C. Madden and C. Myers (eds.): *Discourse and Performance of International Teaching Assistants.* Alexandria, Va.: TESOL. pp. 189–200.

**Yule, G.** and **M. Powers.** 1994. 'Investigating the communicative outcomes of task-based interaction.' *System* 22/1: 81–91.

**Yule, G., M. Powers,** and **D. Macdonald.** 1992. 'The variable effects of some task-based learning procedures on L2 communicative effectiveness.' *Language Learning* 42/2: 449–77.

# INDEX